The South Pacific: Emerging Security Issues and U.S. Policy

John C. Dorrance
Ramesh Thakur
Jusuf Wanandi
L.R. Vasey
Robert L. Pfaltzgraff, Jr.

Special Report
1990

A Publication of the
INSTITUTE FOR FOREIGN POLICY ANALYSIS, INC.
Cambridge, Massachusetts, and Washington, D.C.

 BRASSEY'S (US), Inc.
Maxwell Macmillan Pergamon Publishing Corp.

Washington New York London Oxford
Beijing Frankfurt Sao Paulo Sydney Tokyo Toronto

Brassey's (US), Inc., Press Offices:

U.S.A. (Editorial)	Brassey's (US), Inc. 8000 Westpark Drive, 4th floor, McLean, Virginia 22102 USA
(Orders)	Attn: Order Dept., Macmillan Publishing Company Front and Brown Streets, Riverside, NJ 08075
U.K. (Editorial)	Brassey's (UK) Ltd. 50 Fetter Lane, London EC4A 1AA England
(Orders)	Brassey's (UK) Ltd. Headington Hill Hall, Oxford OX3 0BW, England
PEOPLE'S REPUBLIC OF CHINA	Pergamon Press, Room 4037, Qianmen Hotel, Beijing, People's Republic of China
FEDERAL REPUBLIC OF GERMANY	Pergamon Press GmbH, Hammerweg 6, D-6242 Kronberg, Federal Republic of Germany
BRAZIL	Pergamon Editora Ltda, Rua Eça de Queiros, 346, CEP 04011, Paraiso, São Paulo, Brazil
AUSTRALIA	Brassey's Australia, P.O. Box 544, Potts Point, N.S.W. 2011, Australia
JAPAN	Pergamon Press, 5th Floor, Matsuoka Central Building 1-7-1 Nishishinjuku, Shinjuku-ku, Tokyo 160, Japan
CANADA	Pergamon Press Canada, Suite No. 271, 253 College Street, Toronto, Ontario, Canada M5T 1R5

Library of Congress Cataloging-in-Publication Data

The South Pacific.

(Special report/Institute for Foreign Policy Analysis, Inc.)
1. South Pacific Ocean Region—Strategic aspects.
2. United States—Military relations—Oceania.
3. Oceania—Military relations—United States.
4. United States—Military relations—Australia.
5. Australia—Military relations—United States.
6. United States—Military relations—New Zealand.
7. New Zealand—Military relations—United States.
I. Dorrance, John C. II. Series: Special report
   (Institute for Foreign Policy Analysis)
UA875.S68   1990   355'.03309   90-1771
ISBN 0-08-037454-9 (Brassey's)

First Printing 1990
Printed by Corporate Press, Inc., Landover, Maryland.

Contents

Preface

Although U.S. interests in the Pacific Rim have increased, the focus of American attention has not extended to the South Pacific, in sharp contrast to the abiding importance attached to the strategically vital triangle of the North Pacific, the point of a geo-strategic intersection of China, Japan, and the Soviet Union. Such a prioritization in U.S. policy is understandable, for in the North Pacific the Asian rim approaches in geography the northernmost reach of the North American continent, and specifically Alaska. Moreover, China, Japan, and the Soviet Union, in close proximity to each other and as vital actors in the Asian-Pacific area, hold the key to regional power balances and to the future of U.S. security interests on the Pacific Rim.

Nevertheless, the importance of the South Pacific has grown in recent years for a large number of reasons, as discussed in this Special Report. Spanning a vast maritime area and encompassing continental Australia, together with a large array of islands and mini-states with which the United States and other powers have had a variety of dependency relationships, the South Pacific will loom larger in American policy as we move toward the year 2000. While developing their own economies, states in the region will take an increasing part in the evolution of the Asian-Pacific area. The region's indigenous actors are likely to attempt to minimize outside power influence, while becoming at the same time more fully integrated into the patterns of Asian-Pacific economic interaction. At the same time, the interests of Asian rimland powers, including China, Japan, and the Soviet Union, will be directed increasingly toward the South Pacific in the next decade. In light of such changes, an integrated assessment of the South Pacific as an arena for U.S. policy, within the context of American global strategy, is necessary as the United States projects its policy interests and priorities toward the end of this century and into the next.

This work is published in two Special Reports, the first of which was designed to survey the strategic setting and to examine major political, economic, and military trends. This second Special Report, published separately but as a part of this project, has as its focus present and emerging regional security issues with an emphasis on American strategic interests and objectives. The purpose of both Special Reports is to provide an assessment of policy options and implications for the United States. Both have been produced as a joint effort of the Institute for Foreign Policy

Analysis and the Pacific Forum, CSIS, of Honolulu, Hawaii. Special thanks are given to the Earhart Foundation and the John M. Olin Foundation for support to the Institute for Foreign Policy Analysis for these Special Reports.

Robert L. Pfaltzgraff, Jr.
President
Institute for Foreign Policy Analysis, Inc.

L. R. Vasey
President
Pacific Forum, CSIS

Executive Summary

Scattered over some 88 million square kilometers of the Pacific Ocean, the islands of the South Pacific today comprise thirteen independent states and eight dependent territories, but have a land area smaller than that of Texas and a population of less than six million, 3.6 million of whom are inhabitants of one state, Papua New Guinea. Most island states are handicapped by few natural resources, scarce and infertile land, and the continual threat of natural disaster. Only Papua New Guinea, Fiji, and minuscule Nauru, and possibly the Solomons and Vanuatu, appear to have a resource base offering hope of future economic self-sufficiency; most other states and territories are likely to be aid-dependent for the foreseeable future. Nevertheless, the region's political life has generally been stable and largely free of discord. Democratic institutions emerged in most states and the region's human rights record is without parallel elsewhere in the Third World. Nearly all island state governments have a pro-West orientation; only one, Vanuatu, has joined the nonaligned movement.

For the purposes of this study, these twenty-one political entities include five that lie entirely north of the equator: Guam, and the four that emerged from the U.S.-administered "strategic" UN Trusteeship, namely Palau (or Belau), the Commonwealth of the Northern Marianas, the Federated States of Micronesia, and the Marshall Islands. The latter two are independent states, in "free association" with the United States; the other three remain in a dependent status. South of the equator, there are five additional dependent territories: tiny Tokelau, which has chosen to remain New Zealand's last dependency in the region; French Polynesia, New Caledonia, and Wallis & Futuna, which are considered integral parts of France; and American Samoa. The other eleven independent states of the South Pacific are Fiji, Kiribati, Nauru, Papua New Guinea, the Solomon Islands, Tonga, Tuvalu, Vanuatu, Western Samoa, the Cook Islands, and Niue. The latter two have a "free association" status with New Zealand.

Close American bonds to the South Pacific were forged in World War II when the islands became vital strategic "stepping-stones" in the Pacific war leading to Japan's defeat. Although the American military presence in the islands was overwhelming, it left an enormous reservoir of goodwill toward the United States. However, U.S. inattention to the newly independent South Pacific states and perceived insensitivity toward their concerns and interests resulted in considerable depletion of that reservoir of goodwill in the 1970s and throughout most of the 1980s.

In the decades following the Pacific war, Washington's priorities shifted to commitments and issues in other parts of the globe. The development of the South Pacific was left largely in the hands of Australia, New Zealand, France, and Britain. The American diplomatic presence in the South Pacific was negligible, and bilateral U.S. development assistance to the states south of the equator was non-existent prior to the late 1970s. The single major security development was the conclusion in 1951 of the ANZUS pact between Australia, New Zealand, and the United States. ANZUS has provided a security umbrella over the region, and a framework for political cooperation related to shared strategic and political interests.

As the decolonization of the South Pacific progressed, an informal division of labor emerged between the ANZUS partners: The United States focused on its areas of influence and presence in the North Pacific islands, while Australia and New Zealand focused on the South Pacific. The basic strategic concern of all three partners was to assure that the region remained under Western influence and control, and that a Soviet military or political presence was excluded. The latter objective, "strategic denial," was to foreclose the possibility of the islands ever again being used by an adversary to interdict critical Pacific air and sea lanes of communication.

Defense Cooperation

The United States has developed small but welcome defense cooperation programs with Papua New Guinea, Fiji, and Tonga, although that with Fiji was terminated following the 1987 coups. Although there may be scope for some expansion of U.S. defense cooperation in the South Pacific, it is important not to compete with or disrupt long-standing and broader linkages between South Pacific states and Australia and New Zealand. The United States also has responsibility for the defense of the Micronesian states in the North Pacific that are in free association with it. U.S. military "civic action" teams additionally have played a minor but welcome role in island state public works projects, and have also provided major disaster relief following typhoons.

In the South Pacific, Australia and New Zealand have developed close defense links and commitments to most island states—a region of vital strategic significance to each nation. Canberra and Wellington also accept the possibility that an island state government, under domestic siege or other internal crisis, might request their armed intervention, or that they might need to use military forces to evacuate their nationals in an emergency situation.

The United States, Australia, and New Zealand—as well as Japan and other East Asian allies and friends—attach high strategic importance to the region. The island states and territories straddle or are proximate to the air and sea lanes of communication that link the rim nations; these lanes carry nearly one-half of all American foreign trade, and connect the United States to five of its seven alliance relationships. Preservation of freedom of navigation and the security of these trans-Pacific routes thus is a vital national interest for nearly all the Pacific rim nations, and also for island states dependent on export-import trade.

Regional Issues

In contrast to the ANZUS allies' focus on strategic concerns in the South Pacific, the regional states see the main problems as economic insecurity, marine resources encroachment, environmental pollution, nuclear weapons tests, and residual colonialism. All island states and territories have narrowly-based economies. With the exception of Fiji and Nauru, all are heavily dependent on external development assistance and budget support grants for maintenance of even minimal levels of services and physical infrastructure essential to the welfare of their peoples and thus for political stability. With few exceptions, aid dependency is actually increasing while external assistance levels and GDP growth rates are either static or in decline. All island states seek higher levels of foreign investment and new markets for their products, but the potential in these areas is limited. A further problem is unplanned urbanization and accompanying high levels of unemployment and crime. These developments are eroding traditional cultures and their social discipline restraints, with uncertain consequences for the region's future stability. As a result of these economic problems, some states have been reassessing and realigning their foreign policies—including reinforcement and expansion of economic relationships—in an ongoing search for economic security or at least diversification of aid dependency.

Some activities of external powers, principally the United States, France, Japan, and Taiwan, at times have been seen as threatening by island states. As one example, for ten years through the mid-1980s, the American Tuna Boat Association was accused of "poaching" the tuna resource of island state exclusive economic zones. Economically distressed island states bitterly resented and criticized the United States for its slowness in taking corrective action, and the controversy eventually eroded U.S. efforts to block Soviet regional access. Although a 1987 fisheries convention resolved the issue and provided generous financial terms in return for U.S. fishing access, the problem already has reinforced an existing perception of American insensitivity to regional concerns. More recently, Japanese and Taiwanese driftnet fishing has been seen as a serious threat to the region's marine resources and prompted regional state complaints.

Another major regional concern has been that of environmental pollution. Pacific island peoples rely heavily on the sea for food, while the foreign exchange earnings of many states are dependent upon the rich tuna resource of their surrounding exclusive economic zones. The seas also are a major element in the vital tourist trade. For these reasons, the South Pacific Regional Environmental Programme was formulated to protect the marine environment against pollution from land-based sources, harmful seabed activities, and hazardous waste disposal.

Nuclear issues are a related regional political and environmental concern. With the termination of American and British nuclear testing in the Pacific in the early 1960s, French testing has become the catalyst for antinuclear sentiment throughout the South Pacific. France, in response, continues to assert that its requirement for nuclear testing in French Polynesia remains non-negotiable, although since 1988 it has demonstrated new flexibility and sensitivity with respect to other issues.

The 1985 Treaty of Rarotonga, which established the South Pacific Nuclear Free Zone (SPNFZ), is aimed primarily at French nuclear testing. Thanks to Australian efforts, the treaty was crafted to assure consistency with U.S. regional security interests and criteria for adherence to nuclear-weapons free zones. All nuclear powers were invited to respect the provisions of the SPNFZ by adhering to treaty protocols. The Soviet Union and the PRC have adhered. France refused since such action would require a close-down of its Pacific nuclear-test site. Britain and the United States have publicly affirmed that SPNFZ does not conflict with their regional security interests and requirements, but declined to adhere on the basis that such action could promote greater pressure for nuclear-weapons free zones in other areas (e.g., Southeast Asia) where there would be significant damage to Western security interests. The American decision was deeply resented in the region, and the Soviets have with some success exploited the U.S. position and its contrast to that of Moscow's adherence.

Colonialism as an issue in the South Pacific largely disappeared during the 1970s and 1980s, except for the French territories of New Caledonia and French Polynesia. France has been under regional pressure for years to grant independence to New Caledonia. The United States, caught between its vital interests in Europe and regional interests in the South Pacific, sought to remain disengaged and limited itself to vaguely worded expressions of support for the principle of self-determination. The net result was a regional impression of tacit U.S. support for the French position. A solution to this problem may have been found. In 1988 the newly elected Socialist Rocard Government in Paris crafted with all parties in New Caledonia an accord that provides for major political, economic, and social development programs leading to an act of self-determination in 1998. All regional governments and the United States have endorsed the above accord. In the near future, however, similar problems could emerge in French Polynesia, France's nuclear test site, where a majority seeks higher levels of self-government and a potentially violent minority favors independence.

The best outcome, from U.S., Australian, New Zealand, and regional state perspectives, might be an independent New Caledonia with continuing close relationships with France; a self-governing French Polynesia with close links to France—perhaps a form of free association similar to that of the Micronesian states with the United States; and a continuing French presence through development assistance, participation in the South Pacific Commission and other regional institutions, and stabilizing political ties with its former territories.

The Former Trust Territories and U.S. Strategic Interests

For the United States, the evolution of the Trust Territory of the Pacific Islands to self-determination and self-government has been relatively smooth, with one exception. The Northern Mariana Islands have entered into a commonwealth relationship with the United States following a UN-observed act of self-determination. The Marshall Islands and the Federated States of Micronesia have each entered into a free association relationship as sovereign, self-governing states responsible for their internal and foreign affairs, but with defense responsibility delegated to the United States. Either state can unilaterally terminate the relationship in favor of full independence.

Palau, the last remaining element of the Trust Territory, in seven acts of self-determination over seven years, has also opted for free association, but always with a majority less than the 75 percent mandated by its constitution. That unique majority is necessary to override constitutional "nuclear-free" provisions that are in conflict with the free association arrangement's delegation of defense authority to the United States. A political alternative to free association might be independence for Palau, along with a close treaty relationship with the United States which protects fundamental U.S. security interests, for example, exclusion of any third party military presence.

There are no significant internal or external pressures for "decolonization" of the U.S. territories of Guam or American Samoa. Both wish to retain close political links with the United States. However, the former seeks commonwealth status and higher levels of self-government, and similar pressures may emerge in the future in American Samoa.

All of the above areas of U.S presence or influence, with the possible exception of American Samoa, are of actual or potential strategic significance. The Kwajalein Missile Range Facility in the Marshall Islands will remain essential so long as there is a need to test ICBMs. It also is a critical element in the ongoing development of the Strategic Defense Initiative. The same facility and one in the Northern Mariana Islands are also part of a major space-tracking system essential to the detection of Soviet satellite launches. Guam's air and naval facilities are an important element in the deployment of U.S. forces in the Western Pacific. In the event of loss of access to facilities in the Philippines, some operations could be transferred there, and to Palau and to Saipan and Tinian in the Northern Marianas. However, political restraints, cost factors, the absence of large and skilled work forces, and land-mass restraints preclude transfer of most major operations, for example, those of Subic Bay.

Soviet Interests and Objectives

Glasnost, perestroika, the ongoing collapse of the Soviet empire, lessening East-West tensions, and a decline in the threat of global conflict are all reality. Nonetheless, the Soviet Union will remain the West's primary strategic/diplomatic competitor and its most dangerous potential military adversary. Fortunately, the Soviet Union's ability to project naval power into the South Pacific is limited by a number of factors, including lack of a basing structure and port access. Nevertheless, the Soviet Union maintains a formidable Pacific military capability, particularly in the area of submarine warfare. In his July 1986 Vladivostok speech, Gorbachev asserted that the Asia-Pacific area is of growing strategic importance to the Soviet Union.

Soviet diplomacy under Gorbachev has assumed a more innovative character in which ideology is given less prominence and emphasis is placed on improving the Soviet Union's political image in the region. Since 1986 Moscow has pursued Pacific islands policies oriented toward issues of concern to regional states: support for New Caledonia's independence (while the United States appeared indifferent or pro-French); support for the South Pacific Nuclear Free Zone and adherence to the protocols of the Treaty of Rarotonga (while Washington refused to adhere); and political and psychological exploitation of U.S. differences with New Zealand over the latter's nuclear-free policies. The Soviet Union also has initiated new cultural exchanges, trade union liaison arrangements and training programs, and visits by Pacific islanders to the Soviet Union and Eastern Europe. The first Soviet diplomatic presence in the Pacific islands was established early in 1990 with an embassy in Papua New Guinea.

Soviet strategic and political objectives in the Pacific islands parallel those in many other regions: erosion of U.S. and other Western political influence, promotion of island state nonalignment, and restriction of U.S. regional naval and air access. On balance, the pursuit of these objectives thus far has been marked more by failure than success. The region's political and cultural environment is such that any future Soviet successes in these areas are likely to result primarily from Western indifference or insensitivity to the interests and concerns of the island states, and from the activity of regional Soviet surrogates (e.g., Marxist and other leftist Australian and New

Zealand trade unions) and others who independently pursue objectives congruent with those of Moscow. Nevertheless, the United States and its regional friends and allies cannot afford to view with complaisance Soviet challenges to their interests in the Pacific islands.

The Importance of Economic Assistance

A major challenge for the island states is that of competition for an adequate share of finite global development assistance resources. Aside from their own need for higher levels, they face several fundamental problems. First, traditional Western donors increasingly face resource restraints of their own which limit the potential for increasing present levels of assistance—or even maintaining present levels. Second, the United States and West European donors are faced with competing higher priorities, for example, aid to Eastern Europe and Central America. Third, a major political lever of the past is becoming increasingly ineffectual. To some degree U.S., and also Australian, aid and other attention to the Pacific islands has been driven by a need to counter a perceived Soviet threat. Declining threat perceptions now assure lower levels of concern regarding Soviet activities. These factors give added weight to the importance of new sources of aid, for example, Japan, but also potentially some other Asian nations.

Hopefully, traditional donors will realize that their interests are well served by providing adequate levels of economic aid to the Pacific islands. It is the only Third World region that generally shares and practices democratic and free enterprise values, and which gives full practical recognition to human rights. Fiji presently is an aberration, but probably a temporary one. Successful evolution of the political status of the French territories and Palau will eliminate the only remaining significant exceptions to independence or self-government. But even with these exceptions, the region is blessed by an absence of single-party repressive dictatorial regimes and of Marxist or other controlled economies. The ability of the island states to sustain this enviable record, and thus the prospects for a continuing pro-West orientation is, however, in large degree dependent upon their ability to meet the legitimate expectations of their peoples—a requirement that mandates continuing high levels of donor assistance, as well as concerted efforts to promote higher levels of private sector investment and trade, with the long-term objective of reducing levels of aid dependency.

Recommendations

Despite some erosion of goodwill toward the United States, the latter is still held in remarkably high regard within the region. Indeed, most island states seek higher levels of U.S. diplomatic presence and dialogue, U.S.

investment and trade, and U.S. educational opportunities. In that context there were constructive adjustments in U.S. policy toward the South Pacific in 1988 and 1989. The U.S. diplomatic presence has been increased, a modest aid program for the states south of the equator has been expanded somewhat, and in general there has been a higher level of political attention, dialogue, and policy sensitivity. However, much remains to be done, and a small additional investment in sensitivity and resources can reap major dividends for U.S. and other Western interests.

Each of the contributors to these two volumes on the South Pacific not only has addressed the diverse forces shaping the future of the Pacific islands, but also has assessed policy implications and options for the United States. Without suggesting that all authors would necessarily endorse each of the recommendations set forth below, an effort has been made to summarize the principal policy suggestions that emerge from the various papers.

- High priority should be given by the United States to developing a more adequate understanding of the changing national aspirations of political leaders and other elites in the island states and remaining dependent territories.

- U.S. diplomatic activity in the South Pacific should include more frequent visits to the region by high-ranking U.S. officials, and more invitations to senior island state leaders to visit Washington. Of particular importance, the United States must (as it did in 1989) take full advantage of the South Pacific Forum's offer to join in a dialogue with Forum heads of government annually on the pattern of the ASEAN post-ministerial meetings.

- To promote greater understanding between societies, Washington should expand educational exchanges, as well as USIA programs which fund travel to the United States by island political, labor, academic, and media leaders.

- An effort should be made to increase and diversify trade between island states and the United States, including exploration of the possibility of "free-trade" entry into the United States of island state products on the pattern of Australia's and New Zealand's SPARTECA arrangement and the U.S. "Caribbean Initiative."

- Similarly, American private sector investment in the South Pacific should be encouraged through existing governmental mechanisms that have proved effective in other regions.

- Given the high level of Australia's and New Zealand's economic interests and involvement in South Pacific island states, major U.S. trade and investment initiatives should be developed in consultation with Canberra and Wellington.

- U.S. development assistance in the South Pacific should be increased modestly to match more nearly the level of U.S. strategic and political interests in that region. Current efforts to move away from regional projects to bilateral programs should be continued. That strategy is essential vis-a-vis island state sovereignty sensitivities and related U.S. political objectives.

- Regionalism and strong regional institutions well serve both regional state and Western interests. Although U.S. influence in this area is limited, initiatives that reinforce regional cohesion and cooperation should be encouraged and supported.

- In particular, the United States should take its participation in the South Pacific Commission more seriously with higher levels of representation and expertise.

- Island state internal stability crises may emerge in which a government may request external military assistance. In the South Pacific it is far more appropriate that Australian or New Zealand forces, rather than those of the United States or other major external powers, cope with such emergencies. However, in extreme cases, the United States should be prepared to provide logistics or other support, if requested.

- Limited U.S. defense cooperation with South Pacific island states possessing security forces should be continued, but not expanded to the point where it competes with Australian and New Zealand programs. U.S. military "civic action" public works projects and disaster relief are greatly appreciated by the island states and have had considerable favorable impact. These programs should be increased.

- Present efforts to maintain port and airfield access in the South Pacific are critical and should be continued through diplomatic and defense channels.

- Nuclear issues will remain a dominant regional concern requiring the utmost discretion and tact, including a periodic serious review by the United States of its position on adherence to the SPNFZ protocols.

- Moderate Western trade unions, but particularly those in Australia, New Zealand, and the United States, should be encouraged to increase their efforts to counter Marxist and other leftist trade unions operating in the Pacific islands as surrogates for the Soviets. Similarly, the International Confederation of Free Trade Unions should be encouraged to play a more active role in countering the regional activities of the World Federation of Trade Unions, a Soviet front organization.

- The issue of the future status of Palau, the last element of the Micronesian trusteeship to be "decolonized," should be resolved at an early date. While Palauans must resolve the constitutional issues blocking their preference for free association with the United States, the United States should seek ways to facilitate that process while protecting both Palauan and U.S. interests.

- Although the future of the U.S. territories (Guam and American Samoa) is not a regional decolonization issue, that could change in the absence of an adequate Washington response to Guam's desire for commonwealth status and higher levels of self-government, but for continuing U.S. sovereignty. U.S. interests, including that of support for the principle of self-determination, thus require early resolution of Guam's future status.

- To the extent practicable, and if desired by all parties, the United States could provide assistance to New Caledonia during its transition period. U.S. educational opportunities could be provided to New Caledonia's Kanaks, and U.S. investment in Kanak development projects in New Caledonia could be encouraged. These measures would help counter present negative Kanak images of the United States.

- The United States will be faced with an increasingly nationalistic and independent-minded Australia which also will become more and more important as a major regional power. Continued high levels of official dialogue will be of increasing importance to the relationship. However, that dialogue must be strengthened by still higher levels of effective public diplomacy directed at Australian public understanding of U.S. interests and positions, and of the importance of the alliance relationship to both nations.

- Mutual perceptions and understanding of the United States and Australia should be improved, both through new private-sector linkages (business councils and other nongovernmental binational cooperative bodies) and through support of American and Australian studies centers at universities in both countries.

- Despite New Zealand's disruption of the ANZUS alliance with its nuclear-free policies, U.S. and New Zealand interests and objectives in the South Pacific generally remain common or compatible. In these circumstances, U.S. policy goals in the region would be well served by restoration of normal diplomatic and other dialogue with Wellington, and closer cooperation in the South Pacific.

- The United States, Australia, France, and New Zealand should more closely coordinate their policies and actions in the region, and should seek to integrate Japan into these Western consultative processes.

- The Department of State should give higher priority to training specialists in Australian, New Zealand, and Pacific islands affairs, and to utilizing effectively these specialists up to the Deputy Assistant Secretary of State level. The establishment in 1989 of a Deputy Assistant Secretary position responsible for that region is a major organizational improvement with respect to management of U.S. relations with the South Pacific.

U.S. Strategic and Security Interests and Objectives in Australia, New Zealand, and the Pacific Islands

by John C. Dorrance

Australia and New Zealand

The United States has few closer relationships than that with Australia. Shared history and political values, similar national origins and cultures, trade and investment links, and an alliance forged in wartime assure a unique affinity and a broad range of shared national interests and objectives. New Zealand, before its disruption of the ANZUS alliance in 1985, was similarly a valued regional ally.

The relationship's core since the Pacific war has been mutual security. With the demise of British power in the Pacific, Australia and New Zealand looked to the United States for security—the origins of the 1951 ANZUS pact. The United States in turn has looked upon its ANZUS partners, especially Australia, as the linchpin of Western security in the Southwest Pacific and the most reliable of allies. (In addition to their proportionately extraordinary contributions in World Wars I and II, and in Korea, Australia and New Zealand were the only Western nations to support the U.S. effort in Vietnam with troops.)

Ironically, the very reliability of the relationship during the 1960s and 1970s generated a tendency in Washington to take it for granted. Weak consultative processes and the resulting insensitivity of ignorance eroded the linkage. Generational change also has had its impact; Australians and New Zealanders who experienced the origins of ANZUS for the most part are no longer molders of public opinion. At the other end of the relationship few Americans are conscious of Australia, except with respect to sports, exotic marsupials, and Crocodile Dundee. The images are positive but superficial.

Nonetheless, there has been growing awareness in Washington of Australia's importance, particularly since New Zealand's disruption of ANZUS. Intergovernmental consultative processes and defense cooperation are now at the highest levels since 1945. In Australia, public support for the alliance currently is strong and assures bipartisan political party support, although there are troublesome trends.

1

U.S. Strategic and Security Interests

U.S. interests with respect to Australia are multiple and in some cases critically important for broader Western alliance security. Australia's location between the Indian and Pacific oceans and close to the Indonesian archipelago gives it enormous strategic importance, particularly with regard to vital sea lanes. In a variety of Indian Ocean and South Pacific contingencies, U.S. air and naval access to Australia would be essential, including in particular for ship refueling, replenishment, and repair.

From a global perspective, Australian-American "joint facilities" in Australia (often called "American bases," even though jointly operated and managed) are vital not only for the United States and Australia, but also for NATO and other allies. A naval communications facility provides a primary means for U.S. and Australian communication with submarines in the Indian and Pacific oceans. Others, mainly satellite down-links, are essential to verification of arms control agreements, early warning of Soviet missile launches, and sophisticated intelligence collection. For a variety of technical reasons, it would be extremely difficult (perhaps impossible in the short term) to site these facilities elsewhere. Their importance for Western security and for arms control progress cannot be overstated.

Australia also has the most sophisticated allied defense forces in the Southern Hemisphere. Current Australian defense policy is directed at achieving self-reliance for a variety of regional contingencies while recognizing that a broader conflict would require, as in the past, cooperation between Australian and U.S. forces. Either global or major regional conflict could trigger mutual ANZUS obligations with a division of labor: for example, Australian forces have a capability for and a significant role in antisubmarine warfare and other missions in the protection of sea lanes in an area embracing almost 10 percent of the globe's surface. For these reasons, and especially during the past five years or so, extremely close relationships have developed between Australian and U.S. forces to assure inter-operability of forces, equipment, and doctrine.[1]

Australia and New Zealand play a positive leadership role in their region, but especially with regard to the Pacific islands. While quick to assert they are not surrogates for the United States, shared fundamental regional interests assure that their influence is generally directed at objectives also serving U.S. interests. They also have traditionally played a significant security role in Southeast Asia and still participate in the Five-Power Defense Arrangement with Malaysia and Singapore.

Australia additionally is of global strategic importance because of its mineral resources: 27 percent of the world's uranium reserves and mas-

---

[1] For a current statement of Australian defense strategy, force planning, and threat perceptions, see Australian Department of Defense, *The Defense of Australia 1987* (Canberra: Australian Government Printing Service, 1987).

sive reserves of iron, coal, bauxite, manganese, and other minerals. The Japanese and many other economies are heavily dependent on secure access to them. Beyond the foregoing, Australia is a major American trading partner, and the only significant one in the Asia/Pacific region with which the United States has a favorable trade balance. Nearly 1,000 U.S. corporations have subsidiaries or partners in Australia, and the latter is one of the largest foreign investors in the United States.

There are some differences between Washington and Canberra on broader strategic and arms control issues. For example, Australia opposes the Strategic Defense Initiative as potentially destabilizing to the central balance of forces and favors an early comprehensive nuclear test ban treaty. Nonetheless, there are fewer differences than with most other allies, and Washington and Canberra in recent years have taken great care to assure the above differences and others (e.g., Central America and agricultural trade) have not threatened defense cooperation.

Australian and New Zealand Security Perceptions

Australia's continental size (equal to the U.S. mainland), relatively small population (16 million), geographic isolation from the West, proximity to perceived potential Asian threats, and the lessons of World War II have prompted a traditional reliance on collective security. Australian governments thus accept the need for the Western alliance network, and a corollary obligation to contribute to that system, for example, the joint facilities. However, for some years the more immediate concern has been that of regional threats, the tailoring of Australian forces for such contingencies, and the associated need to cultivate (aside from economic considerations) relationships with the ASEAN states, the Pacific islands, China, and Japan.

That strategy assures Australian regional policy objectives which parallel those of the United States, including denial of regional military access and political influence to the Soviets or other potential adversaries, and promotion of the political stability that serves security interests. New Zealand, far smaller with far fewer resources and much less influence, has a parallel strategy but is less prone to see threats.

The application of the above strategy is most evident in the Pacific islands where Australia and New Zealand participate in most regional organizations, maintain a major diplomatic presence, and are among the largest donors of development aid. Australia in particular has developed close defense relationships with key island states, especially Papua New Guinea and Fiji, but also with Tonga and Vanuatu. (That with Fiji was suspended following the 1987 Fiji military coups.) A major Australian contribution has been provision of patrol boats to most island states which, with other defense cooperation, tends to strengthen island government awareness of regional strategic issues. On a smaller scale, New Zealand has similar relationships with some of the same states. Both assume the possibility, however remote, of a Pacific Grenada and are tailoring forces to respond to such a crisis. Both also maintain, under a long-standing agreement with the United States, maritime surveillance of sea lanes in their region, including, in the case of Australia, much of the Indian Ocean.

Looking to the future, aside from the receding threat of global conflict, Australia perceives several potential if presently improbable threats. Indonesia's confrontation with Malaysia during the Sukarno era, Australia's involvement in that crisis, and Indonesia's forceful seizure of West Irian (the western half of New Guinea island) and Portuguese East Timor have generated in Australia a pervasive uneasiness about that near neighbor. There is concern that re-emergence of Sukarnoism in Jakarta could result in military action in Papua New Guinea triggering Australian involvement, or attempts to close Indonesian archipelago straits essential to Australian trade and security. Underlying that concern are memories of the Japanese thrust into Papua New Guinea in World War II and the associated threat to Australia. There is also worry about the future political directions of some nearby island states and territories. Further afield, there is growing uneasiness about India's regional ambitions, especially given the expansion of the Indian Navy into the region's largest. There also is the long-standing concern regarding Soviet capabilities in the Indian and Pacific oceans, including the Soviet military buildup in Vietnam.

Related to all of the foregoing, Australia attaches the highest importance to an effective U.S. military presence in the Pacific and Indian oceans, and thus continuing U.S. access to defense facilities in the Philippines. For these reasons, Canberra shares U.S. concern that antinuclear sentiment in the Pacific could limit U.S. military access, and condemns New Zealand's nuclear-free policies as an unfortunate precedent.

The present New Zealand government, by way of contrast, perceives few threats and little in the way of a security role beyond neighboring island states. That, coupled to a deeply-rooted nuclear allergy (triggered in the main by the proximity of French nuclear testing), led Wellington to risk the ANZUS alliance by banning access to New Zealand by nuclear-armed and -powered ships. Given U.S. policy to neither confirm nor deny the presence or absence of nuclear weapons on U.S. ships, New Zealand in effect banned the U.S. Navy. That action led the United States to suspend its alliance obligations to New Zealand, in part to demonstrate elsewhere that mutual security treaties are indeed mutual, that is, an ally cannot cease to fulfill its defense cooperation obligations and continue to receive the benefits of an alliance relationship. The United States also ended most defense cooperation and intelligence transfers, and limited New Zealand's diplomatic access in Washington. No longer an ally, New Zealand is now only another distant and small friend. ANZUS in effect has become two bilateral alliances: one between Australia and the United States, and the other between Australia and New Zealand.

Challenges and Threats to U.S. Strategic and Security Interests

Setting aside the low potential for global or regional conflict, primary threats to U.S. interests with respect to Australia and New Zealand relate primarily to certain characteristics of the two countries and to specific elements of our relationships.

In Australia, attitudinal trends (in part a reflection of generational change), as evidenced by opinion polls, suggest there is some ongoing erosion of public support for Australian contributions to global Western security and more specifically for the Australian-American alliance, especially U.S. Navy "nuclear ship" port access and the joint facilities. The latter are perceived as potential nuclear targets. The same polls also indicate declining confidence in the U.S. security commitment to Australia, and a reversal of past attitudes; many Australians now believe the alliance benefits the United States more than Australia.[2]

Coupled to the foregoing is an ever-present political problem: the strong and articulate "hard left" of Australian political life and the related strength of various antinuclear peace groups. Though very much a minority, leftists have significant power through control of a number of key trade unions, and influence within the governing Labor Party, the media, and academia. They are unlikely ever to govern Australia, but they can cause difficulty for specific policies and aspects of defense relationships. Leftist trade union action in 1988 prevented a British aircraft carrier, assumed to be nuclear-armed, from entering Melbourne's harbor. Several years earlier potential union action triggered Australian government refusal of dry-dock access to another British carrier. The foregoing raises the question of the reliability of access to Australian ports by U.S. Navy ships for essential servicing related to any conflict opposed by the Australian left.

Moreover, should U.S. access to defense facilities in the Philippines be denied in the future, it is unlikely that they could or would be replaced by new ones in Australia. Aside from cost factors, the United States is unlikely ever to base major naval and air assets south of the Indonesian archipelago's choke-points and so distant from commitments in the North Pacific. In peacetime, absent direct threats to Australia, it also is questionable whether any Australian government would accept home-porting or semi-stationing of U.S. Navy ships. Beyond probable negative domestic Australian political sentiment, the prolonged presence of nuclear weapons-capable U.S. Navy ships (or aircraft) could be interpreted as an Australian violation of South Pacific Nuclear Free Zone provisions, and of national policy going back to the early 1970s. On the other hand,

---

[2] Poll data obtained from the Office of Research, U.S. Information Agency, Washington, D.C.

Australian Foreign Minister Gareth Evans in early 1989 stated that some functions related to U.S. Air Force operations might be relocated in Australia.[3]

The above realities of Australian political life, driven in part by Australia's Vietnam trauma, impose major political limits on any Australian government's ability to commit forces to foreign contingencies. Illustrative is a comparison of past Australian performance and that possible today. Historically, from the late 19th century through Vietnam, Australia participated almost automatically in every significant conflict involving either the British or subsequently their American ally. Such commitments were part of a strategy of "forward defense," but also pragmatically were seen as insurance premiums—to assure a reciprocal allied response to any threat to Australian security.

The latter assumption came into serious question in the 1970s. Australians interpreted the Guam Doctrine as meaning Australia could not rely on the United States for anything short of global conflict, that is, for the regional contingencies of greatest concern to Australia.[4] That interpretation drove evolution of an Australian defense policy directed at regional threats and maximum self-reliance, and a new Australian reluctance to engage in distant conflicts. However, self-reliance is not self-sufficiency. Canberra has recognized that the ability of Australian forces to cope with regional contingencies requires high levels of defense cooperation with the United States to assure logistics resupply, intelligence flows, and other support short of U.S. armed intervention. Additionally, Australian forces do retain an ability to project air and naval power beyond their immediate regional environment.

Secretary of State Shultz in 1983 attempted to provide reassurance of the reliability of the U.S. commitment: ". . .there should be no doubt that an armed attack on an [ANZUS] ally would require and would receive from the other allies full and prompt fulfillment of the ANZUS security commitment including, when necessary, military support."[5] Other senior officials have emphasized that the ANZUS security commitment applies to all threats, not just global conflict and the Soviets.[6] Yet today many and

---

[3] "We're Capable of Boosting U.S. Help: Evans," *Melbourne Sun*, January 26, 1989, p. 21.

[4] Australia has never recognized that the Guam Doctrine was directed at Asian friends and allies, not ANZUS.

[5] These remarks were delivered by Secretary Shultz at the July 1983 ANZUS Council meeting in Washington during a major review of the ANZUS alliance. The author was present. The statement was repeated and reaffirmed by the Department of State spokesman at a press conference on July 19, 1983.

[6] As one example, Assistant Secretary of State for East Asia and the Pacific Paul Wolfowitz in 1984 said: "Our commitment to our [ANZUS] allies is not limited to any particular threat; it applies to any potential aggressor." Paul Wolfowitz, "The ANZUS Relationship: Alliance Management," paper delivered on June 24, 1984, at Pennsylvania State University. *Current Policy*, No. 592, June 24, 1984, Department of State, Washington, D.C.

perhaps most Australians question any Australian commitment that could lead to involvement in any conflict not directly threatening Australia.

The above trends and forces also exist in New Zealand but have progressed far beyond those in Australia, with the consequent breakup of the ANZUS alliance. A further concern, aside from New Zealand's disruption of ANZUS, is what some perceive to be an uncharted drift toward isolationism and pacifism. Such a trend could do significant damage in the Pacific islands where New Zealand influence remains strong in some areas. If nothing else, New Zealand points up a potential future direction for Australia in the absence of a careful tending by Washington of that relationship.

Although New Zealand no longer has an active ANZUS relationship with the United States, her armed forces nevertheless could be a useful Western asset in any Pacific islands contingency, or for regional sea lane surveillance and protection in a broader conflict. Thus, an ongoing deterioration in those forces, occasioned in some measure by the termination of U.S./New Zealand defense cooperation, is worrisome.

Increased Australian/New Zealand cooperation partially offsets that termination, but is inadequate given practical limitations on the level of Australian cooperation, U.S. restraints on intelligence transfers, and the low level of New Zealand government and public support for their armed forces. Even in Australia, budgetary constraints limit real growth in defense expenditures and inhibit implementation of force modernization policies. Current defense expenditures are about 3 percent of GNP—a respectable figure compared to most NATO allies, but small given Australia's environment and the spectrum of contingencies faced by Australian forces.

Another Australian characteristic is increasing nationalism and public hyper-sensitivity regarding sovereignty and independence of political action. A resultant political imperative of all recent Australian governments is a high need to demonstrate frequently a spirit of "independence," that all policies and actions relating to the American alliance are indeed in the Australian interest and not an automatic response to a U.S. requirement. The foregoing flows in large measure from a perception that Australia's Vietnam involvement was a knee-jerk response to a U.S. requirement. It also reflects a past U.S. tendency to take for granted Australian support of U.S. regional actions. Containment of the problem requires constant high-level dialogue and consultations, and effective U.S. public diplomacy.

Two examples of breakdowns in consultative processes underline their importance. During the 1973 Arab-Israeli war the United States placed the U.S. element at the joint naval communications station in Western Australia on war alert without notifying the Australian government. That action alone brought into public question the underlying arrangements for all joint facilities. In the late 1970s, Carter Administration officials openly discussed possible Australian participation in a proposed Middle East multi-national rapid deployment force—with no prior consultation with Canberra. Suspicion of U.S. intentions flowing from that incident for years afterward complicated legitimate U.S. efforts to engage Australia in joint planning for regional contingencies.

The foregoing incidents highlight yet another problem. To some degree the United States from time to time has taken actions viewed as damaging or insensitive by Australia through sheer ignorance of their impact on Australia. The problem also exists in Australia where general knowledge of the United States is at a higher level, but frequently is distorted negatively by the media and academic institutions, often deliberately.

U.S. agricultural trade policy and legislation also have become a major irritant in recent years. A significant proportion of Australia's economy is dependent on the export of agricultural products in competition with the United States. U.S. subsidy of farm exports is perceived as having seriously damaged the Australian economy. That perception has prompted even some of the most conservative elements of Australian society to urge linking Australian defense cooperation to U.S. performance in agricultural trade. The current Australian government rejects that strategy, but continuation of the issue could in time popularize the concept to the point that U.S. security interests could suffer.

Possible U.S. Responses

(1) Fundamental U.S. interests in Australia appear to be secure at least for the near future. The lessons of the past concerning the importance of consultative processes and dialogue at the governmental level have been heeded. However, those processes often fall short of coordination of Australian and U.S. policies and programs in pursuit of common objectives, particularly with respect to the Pacific islands. Both nations' interests would be served by strengthening such coordination.

(2)The broader problem of superficial or distorted perceptions of each other must be addressed if negative trends are to be contained. Several practical possibilities in this area should be addressed. (a) Unlike most other important U.S. bilateral relationships, there are no significant bina-tional private sector linkages (e.g., the United States-Japan Business Council) which reinforce official relationships through the influence of private sector opinion leaders. Proposals to establish similar Australian-American linkages should be actively encouraged by the U.S. government. (b) Australian studies centers exist at Pennsylvania State University and the University of Texas while a counterpart American studies center is being established at the University of Sydney in Australia. All three can serve the relationship by broadening mutual knowledge and sensitivity.

U.S. agencies involved in education and public affairs should provide program and grant support.

(3) Related to the foregoing, and essential to assure a continuing acceptance of the relevance of the alliance relationship, the United States should dedicate modest additional resources to "public diplomacy" in Australia. To some degree the United States has lost ground in recent years simply because of the inadequacy of existing, mainly human, public affairs resources in that country. As part of that public diplomacy strategy, President Bush should visit Australia. Although Australian Prime Ministers frequently visit Washington, only one serving President, Lyndon B. Johnson, has ever visited Australia. No other key alliance partner has been without a presidential visit for more than 20 years.

(4) Agricultural trade conflicts cannot be fully resolved on a bilateral basis; they are a far broader problem with implications for other alliance relationships as well as for domestic U.S. interests. However, current multilateral efforts to end subsidies and protectionism must be continued and reinforced. The issue is exacerbated by an Australian tendency to exaggerate the impact on Australian trade of U.S. agricultural programs; tensions are compounded by U.S. denials that U.S. programs have a negative impact on the Australian economy. Both positions are flawed. Mutual interests would be well served by less emotion and more effort at establishing at least a common data base on which to address the issue in both multilateral and bilateral forums.

(5) There is no prospect that the present New Zealand Labor government will reverse those policies that destroyed that leg of the ANZUS alliance. There will be elections in New Zealand in 1990 and the opposition hopes to restore the ANZUS relationship. But the depth of popular antinuclear sentiment is such that, even should the conservative National Party win, it will take strong and skilled political leadership to alter current policy sufficiently to permit restored U.S. Navy port access on a basis that would not create negative precedents for other alliance relationships, and that would survive future changes of government. Meanwhile, it is essential that the demonstration effect of current U.S. policy, so important vis-a-vis more crucial alliance relationships, be left intact.

However, some fine-tuning of the present relationship might, without damaging the demonstration effect, limit to some degree deterioration of New Zealand's armed forces—for example, by assuring that there are no constraints on technology and intelligence transfers that would inhibit defense cooperation between Australian and New Zealand forces. Similarly, restraints on diplomatic dialogue that have gone beyond those in other non-alliance relationships might be adjusted to permit a more effective effort at minimizing prospects for drift toward isolationism and pacifism. However, since Australia's own interests are even more directly involved, Canberra should find ways to place greater pressure on Wellington to rethink current national directions.

(6) As to management of the ANZUS relationship and the need to promote continuing acceptance of its relevance, a small ANZUS secretariat headed by a secretary-general could be established in Canberra. This step would give recognition to the fact that the alliance is a Southwest Pacific arrangement, and that Australia is the critical player. Aside from being responsive to Australian nationalism and providing to Australia a further vested interest in the welfare of the alliance, a permanent secretariat could strengthen joint planning and assessments while also providing another channel for promotion of public support. It also might play a subtle role in promoting New Zealand's reintegration.

The Pacific Islands

The Regional Setting

With the close of World War II the Pacific islands rapidly slipped from American consciousness, except for Micheneresque perceptions of the region as a tropical paradise. U.S. bases, except in Guam and Hawaii, were closed. Elsewhere the only significant defense-related activities were nuclear testing between 1946 and 1962 (mainly in the Marshall Islands), and the subsequent development of the Kwajalein Missile Range facility in the Marshall Islands. For nearly 35 years the region was viewed by Washington as a tranquil colonial backwater requiring neither attention nor resources against the backdrop of priorities driven by East-West competition and rising North-South tensions.

American neglect of the region, comprising three distinct cultural and ethnic subregions—Melanesia, Micronesia, and Polynesia—was perhaps natural. All South Pacific colonies (except American Samoa) were administered by allies: Australia, Britain, France, and New Zealand. The North Pacific Micronesian islands formerly controlled by Japan (Northern Marianas, Palau, Yap, Truk, Pohnpei, Kosrae, and the Marshalls) came under U.S. administration in 1947 as a United Nations "strategic" trust territory. Pressures for political change within the region were minimal and peaceful; there were no threats to vaguely defined U.S. interests. However, that equation began to change in the 1960s as the islands entered the decolonization cycle. Since 1962 nine independent states have emerged in the South Pacific while two small former New Zealand territories have entered into free association with New Zealand as self-governing states. France retains three dependent territories while American Samoa remains a U.S. territory.

In the North Pacific the Micronesian trust territory has fragmented and, with the exception of the trusteeship agreement's continuing application to

Palau, has been terminated. The Republic of the Marshall Islands and the Federated States of Micronesia (Kosrae, Pohnpei, Truk and Yap) have entered into free association with the United States as self-governing sovereign states. Both conduct their own foreign affairs and have the right to opt for full independence; the United States has full defense responsibility. The Northern Mariana islands have entered into a closer commonwealth relationship with the United States. Guam remains a U.S. territory, although it too is likely to move toward a commonwealth relationship. Palau may move toward free association, or possibly independence and a close treaty relationship with the United States in the 1990s.[7] In sum, a new galaxy of mini-states has emerged in the Pacific.

If size and population were the sole measures, the Pacific islands would have small claim to outside attention. The 10,000 islands of the region's 21 states and territories embrace only 215,000 square miles of land with a total population of only 5.9 million. Although there are dramatic differences in size (ranging from Papua New Guinea's 180,274 square miles to Nauru's eight), in population (from Papua New Guinea's 3.6 million to Niue's 2,900), in language (1200 separate language groups) and in cultures, there are also many shared characteristics.

Generally, traditional cultures have remained strong, including an almost mystical attachment to land and the surrounding seas. Everywhere Christianity is a major social and political force. In all states a small handful of educated elites dominate public opinion and governmental decisions on issues important to Western interests. In most states politics and the few political parties have little ideological content. Ethnic conflict is generally absent, except in New Caledonia and Fiji where the indigenous populations have become a minority with resultant conflict: insurrection against the French in New Caledonia, and military coups in Fiji to assert ethnic Fijian domination over the Indian community.

---

[7] Although a free association agreement has been negotiated with Palau, and has been aproved by large majorities in seven UN-observed acts of self-determination, a conflict between U.S. defense responsibilities and Palau's constitution has blocked implementation. Some U.S. Navy ships and U.S. aircraft visiting Palau would be potentially nuclear armed, a violation of a constitutional prohibition of the entry into Palau of nuclear weapons. The "nuclear free" clause of Palau's constitution can be overcome by a 75 percent majority in favor of free association in acts of self-determination. However, the majority in all acts thus far has been a few points less. An alternative Palauan remedy is to amend their constitution which requires only a simple majority in three-fourths of Palau's 16 states by referendum. A political alternative to free association might be independence, but also a close treaty relationship with the United States which protects fundamental U.S. security interests, for example, exclusion of any third party military presence. The failure of the seventh referendum on free association (February 6, 1990) to achieve the mandated 75 percent approval may make this option more attractive. However, Palau's "nuclear-free" constitutional provisions probably would apply, with the consequence that U.S. military options in Palau could be severely inhibited.

Only one state, Papua New Guinea, has a current positive trade balance and a reasonable GDP growth rate; most others have nearly static or negative GDP growth rates. With the exception of Papua New Guinea, the Solomons, Fiji, and Vanuatu, none (given present technology) has a material resource base essential to any hope for a future reasonable level of self-sufficiency.[8] Exceptionally high levels of aid dependency everywhere assure high levels of vulnerability to external influences. With several major exceptions, there is little to attract significant foreign invest-ment capital. In most states the economies are a mix of subsistence agriculture, government services and employment, and small private sectors servicing the latter. In many states relatively high levels of literacy and education, growing urbanization and high levels of unemployment, especially among the young, pose serious social and political problems, and fertile ground for extremist movements. Some regional states and territories also are becoming major links in trans-Pacific drug-trafficking.

The islands nevertheless have other characteristics that assure a degree of positive uniqueness. Their peoples and most of their leaders, by Third World standards, have been fundamentally conservative and pragmatic. For the most part, decolonization was achieved without conflict and democratic institutions exist in most states. The island states also have established regional organizations unique in terms of effective political and economic cooperation, and avoidance of ideological conflict or content. Most have retained amicable ties with their former colonial administrators and, with the exception of some aspects of Vanuatu policy, are far more sympathetic to Western than to Soviet interests.

However, that essentially benign situation is changing at an accelerating pace. Generational change is bringing to leadership new elites frustrated with overwhelming dependence on traditional Western links (especially Australia and New Zealand) and prone to explore alternatives not neces-sarily consistent with Western security interests—but also to seek higher levels of U.S. development assistance to diversify their aid dependency.

Fiji, formerly a role model for multi-racial democracy, in 1987 suffered two military coups and the destruction of democratic institutions. The last elected government, Indian-dominated and in office only a few weeks, had embarked on a course toward nonalignment and antinuclear policies similar to those of New Zealand. The future may be bleak. Only the will of Fiji's military to use force to maintain the new status quo will suppress political polarization and unfortunate consequences for Fiji's future political directions and stability. Aside from an embittered Indian community, a

---

[8] One state, tiny Nauru, is economically self-sufficient, but its only resource, phosphate,will be depleted in the 1990s.

significant proportion of the ethnic Fijian community is resentful of the new focus on traditional values and leadership.

New Caledonia has witnessed inter-communal ethnic violence as its indigenous Kanak population seeks independence from France. A 1988 accord between New Caledonia's ethnic communities and France hopefully will lead to peaceful self-determination in the 1990s. But the arrangement is fragile and may be sabotaged by extremists; the potential for renewed insurrection and radicalization of a frustrated Kanak community thus remains present. While no one doubts a French capability to maintain military control of New Caledonia, there remains the question of French political will should that control become too costly in political, financial, and human terms.

Vanuatu since independence has suffered chronic and occasionally violent political instability. Alone among the island states, with Cuban encouragement and support, it has joined the nonaligned movement and developed relationships with Libya, North Korea, and Vietnam. However, recently there has been an erosion of these links and a movement toward closer relationships with the United States.

Papua New Guinea, the region's largest state, has suffered repeated border incursions by Indonesian forces determined to suppress a smoldering indigenous revolt along a common land border. Radicalization of either government could lead to escalation of military action in this area. Such a development, given Australian interests in and defense relationships with Papua New Guinea, could involve Australian forces with a resultant ANZUS alliance obligation implication for the United States. Papua New Guinea also has experienced the instability of "revolving door" government (in part a product of shifting and often purchased political loyalties) and an ongoing secessionist rebellion. Such instability, as well as that in Vanuatu and the Solomons, provides opportunities for mischief-makers.

French Polynesia, the French nuclear test site, may face political turmoil in the 1990s. It has massive social problems, a majority favoring higher levels of autonomy, and a growing minority favoring independence and perhaps prone to violence. Riots in 1987 left the capital, Papeete, looking like a war zone. However, a future French preparedness to grant higher levels of autonomy together with current efforts at social reform could resolve that territory's political problems.

The potential for instability also exists in nearby Tonga where all real power is held by a handful of nobles and an elderly king. Palau, in the North Pacific, has suffered political violence (including assassination of its first President) related to differences over the nature of a future free association relationship with the United States.

Fear of French nuclear testing, resentment of past French policy in New Caledonia, and the bombing by French agents of the Greenpeace *Rainbow Warrior* in New Zealand's Auckland harbor have made France something of a Pacific pariah. Recent changes in French policy toward New Caledonia and increases in French development assistance to island states have softened that perception. Meanwhile, the U.S. image has suffered from guilt by association with French interests and policies.

The region once was described as an "ANZUS lake." Aside from France and at an earlier time Britain, the only external powers with influence and a presence were Australia, New Zealand, and the United States. That, too, is changing. Today, in varying degree, positive and negative, the Soviet Union, Libya, Indonesia, Japan, Taiwan, the PRC, the two Koreas, Vietnam, Malaysia, Singapore, Israel, and West Germany are active in the region. The most positive development has been the recent emergence of Japan as a major source of development assistance. The most negative from a Western perspective has been Soviet entry into the region through fisheries agreements and the forthcoming opening in Papua New Guinea of the USSR's first Pacific islands embassy. Also of concern has been strong evidence of Libyan provision of arms, paramilitary training, political indoctrination, and financing to elements in Vanuatu and New Caledonia. In short, the traditional perception of the Pacific islands as a tranquil colonial backwater no longer stands.

Against the above background the United States entered the era of regional political change with one major advantage: an enormous reservoir of goodwill from the 1941-1945 Pacific War. But no well can be drawn on indefinitely without replenishment. Generational change, U.S. "benign neglect," and U.S. actions on issues important to island states together have sharply eroded images of the United States and the U.S. position. The causes are multiple and synergistic. Above all, there has been the perception and associated resentment of U.S. disinterest in the welfare of the South Pacific, evidenced until the recent past by a token diplomatic presence and a near zero contribution to the development needs of the region. Even today U.S. development assistance to the island states (excluding the Micronesian states in free association with the United States) is less than 4 percent of total economic assistance flows to the region.[9]

A major damaging issue until the recent past was conflict over fishing rights. For many island states the only significant resource is tuna in their oceanic exclusive economic zones. Conflicting positions on jurisdiction

---

[9]The United States is committed to provide about $3.3 billion in grants to the Marshalls, Federated States of Micronesia, and Palau (the latter on implementation of the free association agreement) over 15 years, plus a broad range of federal services. U.S. official development assistance (including economic support fund grants) to South Pacific states was $22 million in FY 1988. However, this includes $10 million in fisheries treaty grant obligations which island states perceive as payment for a resource, not aid. There also are Peace Corps programs in many island states.

over tuna, a migratory species, resulted in American tuna fleets pirating—in the view of the island states and most other nations—that resource. When non-licensed American tuna boats were seized, U.S. law required punitive sanctions against the island state involved. The latter process generated a major crisis in U.S. regional relationships in the early 1980s. The issue was resolved at least temporarily in 1987 with a five-year agreement between the United States and the member states of the South Pacific Forum Fisheries Agency providing for licensing of U.S. tuna boats, catch zones and quotas, and U.S. payment of $12 million annually in fees and grants.[10] But the damage done was significant and was compounded by the U.S. decision in 1987 not to adhere to the protocols of the 1986 Treaty of Rarotonga, which established the South Pacific Nuclear Free Zone (SPNFZ) embracing Australia, New Zealand, and the South Pacific island states. The Soviet Union and the PRC have adhered, while Britain and France have not.

Throughout the region antinuclear sentiment is strong, and not confined to elites. SPNFZ was in some measure intended to ward off pressures for more radical restraints, and a major effort was made to tailor it, primarily at the urging of Australia and Fiji, to satisfy U.S. criteria for nuclear free zones, as well as U.S. regional security requirements. SPNFZ thus only bans the testing and stationing of nuclear weapons in the zone, acquisition of nuclear weapons by zone states, and ocean dumping of nuclear waste. Nuclear powers adhering to the treaty protocols are committed to accept these restraints in their territories within the zone (for the United States, American Samoa), to refrain from using nuclear weapons against states within the zone, and not to test or assist in the testing of nuclear weapons in the zone. The treaty recognizes international law and usage concerning innocent passage and other transit of ships and aircraft, nuclear-armed or not. It also acknowledges that port and air access by nuclear-armed ships and aircraft remains a decision for each signatory. In short, the treaty did no more than codify the existing national policies of most zone states, including Australia.[11]

U.S. officials have stated publicly that SPNFZ does not impair essential U.S. security requirements in the region, and have affirmed that U.S. actions in the zone are not inconsistent with the SPNFZ Treaty. Nonetheless, the United States in 1987 determined it could not adhere to the

---

[10] The United States holds the view that tuna should be managed on a regional rather than a national basis. U.S. tuna fleets thus did not recognize the jurisdiction of island states over tuna in their exclusive economic zones. Seizures of tuna boats violating these zones triggered Magnuson Act trade and aid sanctions. The agreement mentioned above moots the issue since it is between the United States and a regional institution representing the island states.

[11] The restraint on nuclear weapons stationing is interpreted as not affecting U.S. Navy port calls and transits; it requires no breach of U.S. policy to neither confirm nor deny the presence or absence of nuclear weapons on any ship.

protocols, primarily because of concern such action could strengthen sentiment for nuclear free zones elsewhere that would conflict with U.S. security interests.[12] That decision occasioned considerable bitter regional criticism.

Regional nuclear emotions will continue, will be encouraged by the Soviets who have adhered to the SPNFZ protocols, and in due course could threaten U.S. Navy port access in some island states tempted to adopt policies similar to those of New Zealand.

However, the greatest threat to regional stability, and thus to Western regional interests, may be the growing frustration of island elites with overwhelming dependence on foreign economic assistance—primarily from Australia, France, Japan, New Zealand, the United Kingdom, and the European Economic Community. That understandable frustration has encouraged island states to explore alternatives to traditional linkages and provides openings for the Soviets and others less than friendly to Western interests. However, it also explains South Pacific interest in higher levels of U.S. development assistance, as well as a tendency in some areas toward rhetoric and policy actions with little purpose other than demonstration of independence.

The recent emergence of Japan as the region's potentially largest source for economic aid is a positive development. Although regional suspicions of Tokyo's motives assure Japanese caution in attempting to wield more political influence, there can be little doubt the latter will grow.

The Soviet Dimension

Glasnost, perestroika, and lessening East-West tension (but not competition) are now political realities together with a new Soviet interest in the Pacific. The latter is evidenced by Gorbachev's 1986 Vladivostok speech and expanding Soviet activity in the region. However, we do not know how far Soviet internal reform will go, or what impact it ultimately will have on traditional Soviet foreign policy objectives. Any evaluation of U.S. strategic and security interests thus must continue to be based on the assumption that the Soviet Union remains our most dangerous adversary. Indeed, Soviet reform without changes in fundamental Soviet objectives would only assure a far more effective competitor.

In that context, the United States must continue to take into account the fact that the Soviet Union in the past twenty years has developed a formidable Pacific military capability. Their Pacific fleet is now the largest

---

[12]For a full discussion of the U.S. position, see U.S. Congress, House, Committee on Foreign Affairs, *The South Pacific Nuclear Free Zone*, Hearings and Markup before the Committee on Foreign Affairs and its Subcommittee on Asian and Pacific Affairs on H. Con. Res. 158, 100th Congress, 1st Session, June 19 and July 15, 1987.

in the Soviet Navy.   Intensive development of air and naval support facilities at Cam Ranh in Vietnam, coupled to bases in the Soviet Far East, provides a capability to interdict Western air and sea lanes throughout much of the Pacific, including the mining and closing of the critical Indonesian archipelago straits linking the Pacific and Indian Oceans. Although Soviet naval and air activity thus far has been largely confined to the North and Western Pacific, the South Pacific's potential as an alternate route to the Indian Ocean, should the Indonesian archipelago straits be interdicted by mining, has been recognized by the Soviets, who have conducted regional oceanographic and hydrographic research essential to submarine anti-shipping warfare.[13] Offsetting these Soviet capabilities, U.S. and Allied Pacific naval and air assets generally remain superior to those of the Soviets. With the exception of submarine warfare and possibly strategic air operations, the Soviets would have extreme difficulty mounting and sustaining offensive operations at any distance from Soviet Far Eastern waters.

Soviet negotiation of fisheries agreements with two island states, Kiribati and Vanuatu, also has been cause for Western concern. Although neither agreement was renewed after the first year, others are likely and can provide cover for intelligence collection and, with shore access, political involvement.   Though not related to those agreements, there already is (aside from hydrographic/oceanographic research) intensified Soviet intelligence activity in the area, mostly related to the Kwajalein Missile Range and monitoring of U.S. space activity.[14]

Other Soviet activities include efforts, to some degree successful, to influence island elites through a combination of disinformation programs, training of labor leaders, support for antinuclear peace groups, invitations to visit the Soviet Union, and a recent surge of high-level Soviet delegations to the South Pacific.   Much Soviet activity or influence is indirect, often involving hard left Australian and New Zealand trade unions and other groups, including several international Soviet front organizations.   There also are those who for independent reasons have objectives congruent with those of the Soviet Union. A classic example is the alliance of island church and conservative political leaders, trade unionists, and peace groups on nuclear issues.

Soviet strategic and political objectives in the islands parallel those elsewhere: erosion of Western political influence, promotion of island state nonalignment, and termination of U.S. naval and air access within the region.   In the global East-West competition for influence, the Pacific islands are a particularly attractive arena; a risk-free small investment in funds, energy, and sensitivity can generate impressive returns. A possible

---

[13]Data on Soviet military forces obtained from USCINCPAC, Honolulu.

[14]For examples, see Michael Richardson, "Why the Russians are Coming," *Pacific Defense Reporter*, September 1988, pp. 14-16.

restraint on Soviet regional adventurism is the fact that disconnecting Australia from the Western alliance system remains a priority Soviet strategic objective in the Southwest Pacific. Another is their objective of reducing or eliminating Western naval superiority in the Pacific through arms control measures. These objectives may encourage the Kremlin to avoid actions seen as threatening by Australia or the United States.

The Soviets in recent years have demonstrated an understanding of the conservatism and related suspicion of them present in most island societies. They thus focus their initiatives on issues important to the islanders: endorsement of and adherence to the SPNFZ treaty protocols and praise of New Zealand's nuclear-free policies; support in the UN and elsewhere for New Caledonia's independence; offers of trade and joint investment ventures; and oceanographic research related to regional marine resources. They deny any interest in acquiring military access or bases within the region. They also recognize that the absence of Soviet naval activity (not the peacetime capability) in the South Pacific operates to their political advantage. Regional threat perceptions are lowered, thus encouraging the view that a U.S. naval presence is not relevant to the region. The Soviets actively promote the concept that a Western military presence unnecessarily makes the South Pacific a zone of competition and potential conflict.

The Soviets do have legitimate objectives within the region (e.g., access to tuna, and to commercial shipping and trade opportunities) that of themselves pose no threat to the West, so long as they are not co-mingled with intelligence collection or political involvement. There also is little reason to doubt the Soviet claim of no interest in South Pacific military bases. Aside from the point that no island state is likely to welcome one, it is hard to perceive the utility of such a base relative to higher Soviet priorities. In particular, the pursuit of either bases or simple naval access would be counterproductive with regard to objectives such as denial of U.S. regional access, naval arms control, and removal of Australia from the Western alliance system.

It also can be argued that the pursuit of Soviet strategic, political, and economic objectives thus far has been marked more by failure than by success. They have offered little in the way of aid and trade of interest to the region, have aborted two fisheries agreements, have failed to win over any government, and have a lower level of presence, dialogue, and influence than in any other Third World region. Such gains as have been made must be measured from a zero base. In large measure they can be attributed more to the independent activities of Australian and New Zealand leftists, and to opportunities generated by U.S. and other Western (primarily French) insensitivity than to the cleverness of Soviet regional diplomacy. This does not mean there is no potential Soviet challenge or threat, but it does mean that the region's political and cultural environment is such that any major future Soviet successes are likely to flow in considerable measure from inappropriate Western policy or insensitivity.

U.S. Regional Interests and Objectives

The peaking of the decolonization cycle in the 1970s prompted Washington in the late 1970s to re-examine U.S. interests and policies in the South Pacific, a process that had begun earlier in the North Pacific with the commencement of negotiations in 1969 directed at termination of the Micronesian trusteeship.[15] Strategic and security interests were paramount considerations, although different from those of the past. Changes in the character of potential threats, of air and naval requirements, and of defense technology had together largely eliminated the need for "stepping stone" island bases so important in World War II.

Aside from defense interests, political interests were defined. Clearly, the United States has a strong interest in the development of democratic institutions and governments able to serve the political, social, and economic aspirations of island state peoples. Resulting stability in turn serves U.S. security interests. There also is the related interest in the success of regional organizations (e.g., the South Pacific Forum, and the South Pacific Commission) serving the region's needs.[16] Another interest is self-evident: the United States is part of the region by virtue of Guam, the Northern Marianas, and American Samoa, and through its relationships with the Micronesian states.

Economic interests are minimal. Aside from major U.S. investment in mining and petroleum ventures in Papua New Guinea, the only significant interest is in the region's rich tuna resource. Trade levels are minuscule. (Beyond the problem of limited opportunities, U.S. private sector interest in investment and trade is inhibited by a lack of awareness of such potential as exists.) Regional seabed mineral resources may become important in the future, but that depends upon technology and demand not yet present.

U.S. strategic and security interests and objectives in the region are largely derivative of those elsewhere. Aside from the security of Hawaii, the U.S.

---

[15] For further discussion of the evolution of U.S. policy and definition of U.S. interests, see John C. Dorrance, *Oceania and the United States: An Analysis of U.S. Interests and Policy in the South Pacific* (Washington, D.C.: National Defense University Press, 1980).

[16] The South Pacific Forum includes all of the independent and self-governing island states, plus Australia and New Zealand. The Forum heads of government meet annually to address regional political and economic issues. The South Pacific Commission includes all regional states and territories plus Australia, Britain, France, New Zealand, and the United States. The Commission does not address political issues. The South Pacific Bureau for Economic Cooperation promotes development assistance to the region and serves as the South Pacific Forum's Secretariat.

territories, and the Micronesian states, the primary U.S. defense interest is that of secure lines of communication to friends and allies in Asia, to Australia, and through the Pacific to the Indian Ocean. Nearly one-half of U.S. foreign trade transits the Pacific while five of the seven defense agreements to which the United States is a party are in the Asia/Pacific region.

In the above context, the importance of the North Pacific islands is manifest. Guam and the Northern Mariana islands are strategically located and under American sovereignty. However, their small size and the variety of U.S. commitments and potential contingencies assure they can be only one element in a broader regional commitment of U.S. forces.

Palau, the Federated States of Micronesia, and the Marshall Islands, spread across the Pacific between the Philippines and Hawaii, have a limited role with respect to United States security requirements. The free association relationship between the United States and the latter two of these island states, and potentially with Palau, does provide the United States with defense responsibility, but also with significant constraints on military use. However, the Kwajalein Missile Range facility in the Marshall Islands is politically secure and will remain essential so long as there is a need to test ballistic missiles. The facility also is involved in the develop-ment of the Strategic Defense Initiative. The United States has no current or projected basing requirement in the Federated States. In Palau, should the present free association agreement be implemented, the United States would have only limited contingency rights or options: (a) U.S. Navy anchorage in Palau's main harbor and a small nearby land area for support facilities; (b) joint use with civil aviation of Palau's two main airfields and 2000 acres for logistics support purposes; and (c) periodic access to uninhabited areas for occasional training exercises, after consultation with the Palau government.

Contrary to Soviet and peace group disinformation, the United States does not plan to establish a nuclear submarine base in Palau, or store or station nuclear, chemical, or biological weapons in Palau. Aside from restrictive agreements with Palau, the United States has renounced biological weapons and seeks international agreement on abolition of chemical weapons.

Preferably the "Palau options" will never be exercised in full measure, if at all. They are intended for contingencies which hopefully will never materialize, including loss of U.S. access to defense facilities in the Philippines. In the latter situation the strategic importance of not only Palau, but also of Guam and the Northern Mariana islands would increase as potential sites for relocation of some U.S. military activities. However, cost factors, strategic considerations, their small size, the absence of large and skilled work forces, and limited options in Palau assure that little of importance in the Philippines would be duplicated on these islands.

Micronesia, Guam, and the Northern Marianas have strategic importance in yet another sense. In peacetime they lie well to the south of most sea and air lanes across the North Pacific. However, in any Pacific war involving the Soviets, U.S. air and sea movements would shift into that area to minimize Soviet interdiction. For this reason, but also because of the threat that would be posed to areas south of the equator, a primary U.S. objective since 1945 has been "strategic denial"—preventing an adversary from gaining military access to these islands.

In the South Pacific, the primary U.S. strategic concern remains the security of air and sea lanes between the United States and Australia, but also the safeguarding of an alternate route to the Indian Ocean. In peacetime, as previously indicated, most ship movements from the Pacific to the Indian Ocean are through Indonesian archipelago straits or the Strait of Malacca. However, the Soviets have a capability to mine these straits or to interdict shipping through the South China Sea from Vietnam. There is also the potential for regional states to attempt to close these straits or interdict shipping. In any of these contingencies, North Pacific transits to the Indian Ocean could shift to the South Pacific, and then south or north of Australia to the Indian Ocean.

A relatively new U.S. security interest, and a resultant Soviet interest in the South Pacific, may relate to potential development of anti-satellite warfare technology, although current Congressional restraints severely inhibit testing and prevent deployment.[17] Should this change, the optimal location to intercept Soviet satellites following launch is from a triangular ocean area in the South Pacific northeast of New Zealand and 180 degrees opposite Soviet launch sites. As one authority puts it, "control of areas opposite space launch facilities could deny entry and exit to the respective space programs just as control of Gibraltar or the Strait of Hormuz could deny entry and exit to some critical ports."[18] The related essential launch detection capability is provided by an existing U.S. space tracking network, including radar installations on Saipan in the Northern Marianas and Kwajalein in the Marshalls.[19] (A counterpart Soviet anti-satellite capability would require interception of U.S. satellites from Soviet ships in the Indian Ocean west of Australia.)

Other than for the U.S. territories and the Micronesian states in free association with the United States, there are no direct U.S. security

---

[17] For detailed discussion, see Aadu Karemaa, "What Would Mahan Say About Space Power," *Proceedings of the U.S. Naval Institute*, April 1988, pp. 48-49. Also, Richardson, op. cit.

[18] Karemaa, op. cit.

[19] Richardson, op. cit.

commitments to any of the islands.[20] However, for years island states and the ANZUS partners have accepted that ANZUS provides an informal security umbrella over the South Pacific in that an attack on any state in the region could represent a threat to Australia, New Zealand, or the United States. Beyond that consideration, ANZUS commitments can be triggered not only by an attack on the metropole of the partners, but also by an attack or threat of an attack on their forces or territories in the Pacific area. As a hypothetical example, U.S. obligations could be triggered by an attack on Australian forces responding to an island state contingency. In that context, it is essential to bear in mind that the island states have a geopolitical relationship to Australia and New Zealand similar to that of the Caribbean with the United States, but even more so. The island states are astride their lines of communication with the United States, Japan, and other areas to the north, and dominate strategic approaches to Australia and New Zealand.

Despite the absence of formal security relationships in the South Pacific, there has been modest U.S. defense cooperation (exercises, training, and military equipment sales) with Papua New Guinea, Fiji, and Tonga, the only three island states with defense forces. (Defense cooperation with Fiji was suspended following the 1987 coups.) U.S. forces also participate in disaster relief and civic action construction projects throughout the islands.

The requirements of U.S. security interests in the Pacific islands are modest and essentially satisfied by existing arrangements. In the North Pacific, relationships with U.S. territories and with the Micronesian states assure denial of that region to adversary basing or other military activity and provide, within the very real geographic limitations of the islands, such capabilities as can be foreseen as necessary.

In the South Pacific, no U.S. bases are sought or are required. Denial of adversary military access seems likely to be satisfied for the foreseeable future. A corollary ANZUS political objective had been denial of Soviet political influence in the region. Previously cited developments now change that objective to minimizing opportunities for Soviet activity and influence.

An important requirement is access to major island ports and airfields because of their proximity to key lines of communication. In the event of conflict, such access could be essential for defensive antisubmarine warfare. In peacetime, access can be important for allied tracking of Soviet maritime movements, particularly intelligence collectors. With the exception of New Zealand and Vanuatu, U.S. forces currently have reasonable access everywhere.

---

[20]The 1983 Treaties of Friendship with Kiribati and Tuvalu do provide for consultations in the event of a threat to either state, and that neither will provide military bases to third parties without prior consultation with the United States.

Island State Security Concerns

Although most island states understand fundamental Western security requirements, their own perceptions of security are far narrower. With the exception of Papua New Guinea with its land border and associated problems with Indonesia, none perceives direct external military threats. Rather, security concerns are the inadequacies of development assistance and increasing aid dependency; the associated perception of limitations on their political freedom of action; violations of their sovereignty (e.g., piracy of marine resources from island state exclusive economic zones by Japanese, Taiwanese, and, until the recent past, U.S. fishing fleets); insensitivity to regional interests (e.g., U.S. failure to adhere to the SPNFZ protocols, past low levels of U.S. developmental assistance, and Japanese drift-net fishing, a form of marine-life strip-mining); assumed environmental contamination by French nuclear testing; and the potential for ocean dumping of hazardous waste. To the extent that island leaders perceive their security interests threatened by others, they are unlikely to be sympathetic to the security requirements of the latter. Fortunately, this problem has not yet reached unmanageable proportions. But the potential is there as more ideologically motivated and assertive island leaders replace those who emerged in the post-colonial period.

Possible U.S. Responses

Through historical evolution of their respective links to the Pacific islands, an informal division of labor has emerged between Australia, New Zealand, and the United States. The latter has focused its regional links north of the equator while Australia and New Zealand have played the lead Western role in the non-French areas of the South Pacific. The latter is the major problem area for the United States where new challenges coupled to longstanding perceptions of U.S. disinterest and insensitivity threaten U.S. and broader Western interests. Fortunately the area, despite its problems, remains a relatively low-threat environment with many states still receptive to the requirements of primary Western interests. Of particular importance, despite the erosion of the U.S. image, the United States is still held in relatively high regard in most areas. Most island governments seek not only higher levels of U.S. development assistance, but also of diplomatic presence, dialogue, and influence, if only to balance Australian and New Zealand influence. Opportunities do therefore exist to work with regional friends and allies to limit deterioration.

It would be impractical and politically unwise for the United States to attempt to match or displace Australia's or New Zealand's roles in the South Pacific, but a more active secondary role well serves shared interests and objectives. That point has been recognized in Washington in the past several years, resulting in a number of positive moves. The American diplomatic presence in the South Pacific was expanded from two to four embassies in 1988, and in 1989 U.S. representative offices in the Micronesian states were upgraded to full embassy status. Official dialogue with key island governments has been expanded, and so have educational and cultural exchange programs. Development assistance to South Pacific states in 1988 increased almost fourfold to about $22 million. Similar levels are projected for the next several years. A key political decision was to "bilateralize" U.S. development assistance. Previously most U.S. assistance had been channeled through regional organizations and private volunteer groups. That strategy, though cost-effective, was resented by island governments as reflecting disregard for their sovereignty.

These are major steps in the right direction, but the following additional measures would well serve American interests in the Pacific islands.

(1) In an area where personal high-level contact is an essential element of government-to-government relationships, only one South Pacific head of government has made an official visit to Washington. That should change. Of particular importance, the U.S. government must (as it did in 1989) take full advantage of offers by the heads of government of the South Pacific Forum to meet with them annually on the pattern of the ASEAN post-ministerial meetings. The United States must be represented by a prestigious and knowledgeable senior official. It will be particularly important to use this and other opportunities to develop a regular dialogue on both global and regional issues of concern to the South Pacific states.

(2) Related to the foregoing, the United States must take more seriously its participation in the only major regional organization of which it is a member: the South Pacific Commission. U.S. representation, traditionally weak, should be strengthened and include regional expertise.

(3) Although consultative processes between Australia and the United States with respect to the region are a regular feature of that bilateral relationship, there is little in the way of coordination of policies and activities. Coordination of responses to challenges to shared interests needs to be strengthened, and both consultation and coordination extended more thoroughly to other major Western players, particularly New Zealand and France. (Despite New Zealand's disruption of the ANZUS alliance, most U.S. and New Zealand regional interests and objectives remain essentially shared or compatible.) It also is important to assure harmonious integration of Japan's new regional role, including admitting Tokyo as a full partner in the above processes.

(4) U.S. development assistance to the South Pacific, even with recent increases, bears little relationship to the level of U.S. interests in the region or to regional needs. Increases significant in terms of regional expectations and requirements would remain small relative to global U.S. develop-

ment assistance flows; they could be accomplished with fine-tuning of global allocations rather than budget increases.

(5) A major effort should be made to promote American investment in and trade with the Pacific islands. The present lack of American private sector knowledge of and thus interest in limited regional opportunities can be addressed through existing U.S. government programs that have proved effective in other regions.

(6) A generation of political leaders and other elites is emerging which has had little or no contact with the United States. Educational exchange programs in the South Pacific, and U.S. Information Agency programs that fund travel to the United States of island political, labor, academic, and media leaders, should be expanded further. The first steps in this direction have already been taken.

(7) The goodwill earned by U.S. military disaster relief and civic action programs has been important. If possible, these activities should be expanded.

(8) Although the trade-offs involved are difficult to assess accurately, there should be periodic review of the U.S. position on adherence to the SPNFZ protocols. The primary issue will remain whether the "spill-over" effect elsewhere will indeed be more significant than the political gains for U.S. regional interests.

(9) Although it is difficult to perceive an effective practical role for the United States, measures (even if only symbolic) supportive of efforts to achieve a peaceful resolution of New Caledonia's status should be explored. There also should be recognition that the Kanaks are likely to achieve the independence or autonomy they seek. This requires cultivation of the leadership of that community to offset existing essentially negative and often hostile images of the United States. Kanak expressions of interest in American educational opportunities and private sector investment in New Caledonia should be explored and the latter encouraged. These initiatives should be developed in consultation with the French government.

(10) Continuing uncertainty about the political future of Palau not only brings into question the viability of U.S. defense options in those islands, but also has become a regional political embarrassment. While Palauans must resolve the constitutional issues blocking resolution of their future status, the United States should facilitate that process in any ways that are appropriate and are sought by the Palauans.

(11) Finally, to assure greater policy sensitivity and focus for the entire region, the Department of State should give priority to training and using (as it does for other regions) specialists in Australian, New Zealand, and Pacific islands affairs. A few have been trained in the past, but none

recently. None previously trained currently have assignments relating to the South Pacific.

There are no easy responses to some of the above suggestions, especially since implementation of some would require trade-offs between U.S. regional interests and those elsewhere. On the other hand, the investment in attention, and in human and financial resources, would be exceptionally modest relative to the potential gain. Australian concern for inadequate past American attention to the South Pacific was succinctly put by the Australian Ambassador to the United States in 1985: "If you want the South Pacific to become an area where the Soviet Union, Cuba and others of that stripe can find fertile ground . . . on which they can develop activities directly prejudicial to our interest, then continue with a policy of indifference . . . ."[21]

---

[21] From a speech by Ambassador Rawdon Dalrymple before The Asia Society, New York, September 25, 1985.

Nuclear Issues in the South Pacific

by Ramesh Thakur

As a matter of convenience, the South Pacific region may be defined as being coterminous with the membership of the preeminent regional organization, the South Pacific Forum. It stretches some 17,000 kilometers (10,600 miles) longitudinally from Australia and Papua New Guinea in the west to South America in the east, and 7,000 km (4,400 miles) latitudinally from the equator to the Antarctic Ocean (60°S). In addition to the two "metropolitan" countries of Australia and New Zealand, there are nine states which attained full independence between 1962 and 1980: Fiji, Kiribati, Nauru, Papua New Guinea, the Solomon Islands, Tonga, Tuvalu, Vanuatu, and Western Samoa. Another two, Niue (since 1974) and the Cook Islands (since 1965), are self-governing in free association with New Zealand, a status that circumscribes their freedom of maneuver in external relations. The admission of the Federated States of Micronesia and the Republic of the Marshall Islands in 1987 brought the Forum's membership to fifteen.

Somewhat simplistically, the South Pacific can be divided into three broad groupings: Melanesia in the west, Polynesia in the east, and Micronesia in the north. (Fiji's location in Melanesia or Polynesia is problematic: in fact it lies at the geographical crossroads, and half its population is ethnically Indian.) In general, the Melanesians have been more radical in their antinuclear postures, the Polynesians more conservative, and Micronesia has formed part of the U.S. nuclear security zone in peacetime. While the area and population of the ministates and microstates of the South Pacific are very small, their geographical location gives them a strategic, political, and economic importance transcending their size. The South Pacific countries have become increasingly assertive in the view that they should not only have the decisive say in issues affecting their own region, but that they should also be able to express a regional viewpoint on international issues.

An exceptional feature of South Pacific regional institutions is the emphasis on pragmatic political and economic cooperation to the neglect of ideological politicization and conflict. The South Pacific Commission (SPC) was established in 1947 by metropolitan countries with territories in the South Pacific: Australia, Britain, France, the Netherlands, New Zealand, and the United States. The triennial (but now annual) South Pacific Conference representing indigenous interests was given only an advisory role until 1974, when it became the governing body of the SPC. The South Pacific Forum was set up in 1971 as the symbol and instrument of regional decisionmaking. Australia and New Zealand were invited to join in recognition of their geographical and historical links with the island countries and peoples.[1] The possibility of American Samoan membership was rejected at the 1978 Forum meeting in Niue because of the threat to indigenous control by a U.S. dependent territory. The South Pacific Bureau for Economic Cooperation (SPEC) was established by the Forum in 1972. Located in Suva, its activities include research on and coordination of regional trade, economic development, tourism, shipping, fisheries, telecommunications, and other related matters.

The history of the relationship of nuclear weapons use (by U.S. aircraft based on the Northern Mariana Islands in 1945) and testing in the Pacific area has sensitized Pacific peoples to nuclear issues perhaps more deeply than others.[2] More than once, established opinion has been shown to be tragically defective in regard to the long-term effects of exposure to radiation, the time taken for some symptoms to develop, and the slowness of recovery of the environment from radioactive contamination. The Bikini and Enewetak Atolls in the Marshall Islands were the sites of testing from 1946 to 1958. Enewetak inhabitants returned to their atoll only in 1980; Bikini Atoll may remain uninhabitable for another fifty years. Britain tested atomic and nuclear weapons on Christmas Island and on the Australian mainland in the 1950s, and in 1962 permitted U.S. testing on Christmas Island. France continues to test nuclear systems in French Polynesia.

Arising out of this history, today there are six categories of nuclear issues of concern to the peoples of the region: the possibility of the breakdown of the nuclear peace, and the fact of vertical nuclear proliferation among the nuclear-weapons states (NWS) in quantity and quality of nuclear weaponry; horizontal proliferation to the South Pacific region by the acquisition of nuclear weapons by a state in the region; the spread of strategic weapons doctrines and nuclear weapons deployments to the South Pacific; nuclear testing in the South Pacific; facilities in the South Pacific which constitute part of the worldwide infrastructure of nuclear logistics; and environmental anxieties about possible dumping of nuclear waste in the South Pacific. All six concerns were addressed in the South Pacific

---

[1] For more detailed background information on the SPC, South Pacific Forum, economic cooperation in the region, and New Zealand's links with the region, see respectively, Richard A. Herr, "Organisations and Issues in South Pacific Regionalism"; Robert Igara, "Economic Co-operation in the South Pacific"; and R. Alley, "New Zealand and its Connections with the South Pacific"; in Roderic Alley, editor, *New Zealand and the Pacific* (Boulder, CO: Westview, 1984).

[2] See, for example, Jane Dibblin, *Day of Two Suns: U.S. Nuclear Testing and the Pacific Islanders* (London: Virago Press, 1988), and Stewart Firth, *Nuclear Playground* (Sydney: Allen & Unwin, 1987).

Nuclear Free Zone (SPNFZ) established by the Treaty of Rarotonga in 1985. Not surprisingly, therefore, SPNFZ will be a central element in the discussion of regional nuclear issues in this chapter.[3]

World Order

The South Pacific countries are not exceptional in their sense of dis-enchantment with the meager results of global nuclear arms control talks, and in their feelings of impotence at not being able to do anything about the matter. The United States and the Soviet Union cooperated to produce the Non-Proliferation Treaty (NPT) in 1968, signed it at inception, and ratified it simultaneously on May 3, 1970. The two superpowers bound themselves to certain undertakings in the NPT, the preamble to which recognizes a fundamental link between horizontal and vertical nuclear proliferation. The NPT regime was hence a "package deal" whereby non-nuclear states would refrain from acquiring nuclear weapons, and the nuclear-weapon states would dismantle their nuclear arsenals. Article 6 of the NPT in particular obliged the NWS "to pursue negotiations in good faith on effective measures relating to cessation of the nuclear arms race at an early date and to nuclear disarmament."

The NPT came into force in 1970; the 1987 INF Treaty notwithstanding, South Pacific peoples remain unconvinced that the nuclear powers have faithfully fulfilled their obligations under Article 6. A comprehensive test ban treaty (CTB) seems to be no nearer conclusion in 1989 than it was in 1970. Negotiations on reducing strategic arsenals seem to be fitful non-starters which breed international public cynicism about the "good faith" behind them. Arms control talks all too often seem to be guided by a "ratchet effect" strategy, where the pressure for escalation is slackened temporarily precisely in order to increase it in the next round.

Critical opinion in the South Pacific has become increasingly dissatisfied with conventional explanations of the nuclear rivalry and traditional policy responses demanded of allies. Under the Reagan Administration in the first term, the United States was regarded as being as culpable as the USSR because it too was a prisoner of ideological preconceptions and aggressive rhetoric. Mesmerized by esoteric debates about weapons systems, battlefield tactics, and strategic doctrines, the United States seemed to have lost sight of the real issue of human survival, and there was a general sense of "a plague on both your houses" toward the superpowers. Ronald Reagan's second term, characterized by diminished ideological hostility and practical cooperation with Mikhail Gorbachev's Soviet Union, helped to restore some semblance of credibility

---

[3] For two complementary discussions of SPNFZ, see Ramesh Thakur, "The Treaty of Rarotonga: The South Pacific Nuclear-Free Zone," and Greg Fry, "Regional Arms Control in the South Pacific," in David Pitt and Gordon Thompson, editors, *Nuclear-Free Zones* (London: Croom Helm, 1987).

to the superpowers' role as the custodians of nuclear peace. But this was due more to improved perceptions of Gorbachev than Reagan. In a recently published poll, 40 percent of Australians said that the Soviet Union was more interested in arms reductions, with only 28 percent choosing the United States—though only 23 percent of respondents believed that the USSR was more interested in settling international disputes, while 48 percent believed this to be true of the United States.[4]

Many more people have also begun to appreciate the dangers of the paradox of nuclear deterrence. If the West seeks to deter the Soviet Union with nuclear weapons, then it must convince the Soviets that in certain circumstances these weapons will be used. But if in fact nuclear weapons are used, and produce a like response, then even the West is worse off than if it had not relied upon nuclear weapons in the first place. The fact that the South Pacific too would be devastated in the aftermath of a nuclear war between the superpowers is seen to give its inhabitants both the right and the responsibility to speak out on the dangers of nuclearism. Indeed, the region's geopolitical environment means that the most realistic, and the most serious, threat to the security of its nations is posed by the prospect of a global nuclear war. Efforts to lessen the chances of such an outbreak are therefore a direct pursuit of national security interests, not just based on idealism divorced from the real needs of regional nations.

Horizontal Proliferation

The pursuit of nuclear nonproliferation has been a major international concern of our times. In keeping with this theme, no South Pacific country possesses nuclear weapons or has indicated an intent to acquire them. While attempts to bring about arms control regimes and disarmament seek to tackle the level of armaments directly, efforts to establish zones free of nuclear weapons are confidence-building measures undertaken by those who do not possess nuclear weapons. The NPT was an attempt to bring in a global regime to prevent the acquisition of nuclear weapons by non-nuclear-weapon states (NNWS). States in the latter category can adhere to the NPT while accepting a stationing of nuclear weapons on their territories, as long as they do not exercise jurisdiction and control over the weapons. A Nuclear Weapon Free Zone (NWFZ), however, prohibits such stationing of nuclear weapons. The three essential characteristics of a NWFZ are nonpossession, nondeployment, and non-use of nuclear weapons. NWFZs can help to strengthen and promote nonproliferation by providing a means of extending and reinforcing the NPT.

The Treaty of Tlatelolco of 1967 established the first internationally recognized NWFZ in a populated region of the world, namely Latin America. The second NWFZ in an inhabited region was established at the sixteenth South

---

[4] The Melbourne *Age*, October 17, 1988.

Pacific Forum meeting held in Rarotonga, Cook Islands, when Forum countries adopted the South Pacific Nuclear Free Zone Treaty on August 6, 1985. The preamble to the treaty expressed the commitment to world peace, a grave concern at the continuing nuclear arms race, the conviction that every country bears an obligation to strive for the elimination of nuclear weapons, a belief in the efficacy of regional arms control measures, and a reaffirmation of the NPT and its objective to halt nuclear proliferation. The core obligations were contained in Articles 3-7. Each party agreed not to manufacture or otherwise acquire, possess, or have control—or seek to do so—over any nuclear device; not to assist or encourage others to make or acquire nuclear weapons; to prevent the stationing or testing of nuclear weapons on its territory; not to dump radioactive wastes at sea anywhere in the zone, and to prevent such dumping by others in its territorial sea. The boundaries of the SPNFZ generally follow the territorial limits of the South Pacific Forum members, and are based on the "picture frame" (rather than an "incomplete patchwork") approach.

The Treaty of Rarotonga came into effect on December 11, 1986, when Australia became the eighth country to deposit its instruments of ratification with SPEC. The seven countries that had already ratified were Fiji (October 4, 1985), the Cook Islands (October 28, 1985), Tuvalu (January 16, 1986), Niue (May 12, 1986), Western Samoa (October 26, 1986), Kiribati (October 28, 1986), and New Zealand (November 13, 1986). Nauru ratified subsequently on April 13, 1987, the Solomon Islands on January 27, 1989, and Papua New Guinea deposited its instruments of ratification with the Forum Secretariat in Suva on September 15, 1989. The two remaining nonsignatories are Tonga (a Polynesian conservative) and Vanuatu (a Melanesian radical). (The question of the relationship of the Federated States of Micronesia and the Marshall Islands to the treaty is as yet unsettled because of the complicating element of their links to U.S. security policies, which are discussed below.) Prime Minister Bob Hawke of Australia expressed the hope at the 1988 Forum meeting that those countries not yet parties to SPNFZ would become so in the near future.

Superpower Rivalry in the Region

The most serious gap in the SPNFZ regime is the lack of endorsement by the nuclear weapon states. The Treaty of Rarotonga adopted the simple expedient of containing additional protocols for integrating these states into the SPNFZ. Protocol 1 was addressed to France, the United Kingdom, and the United States, and invited them to apply NFZ prohibitions on manufacture, stationing, and testing to their territories within the zone. (The British territory involved is Pitcairn Island; the French territories are New Caledonia, French Polynesia, and Wallis and Futuna; and those of the United States are American Samoa and uninhabited Jarvis Island.) Protocol 2 was addressed to the five nuclear weapon states and contained the negative security guarantees. In it, each NWS party would agree not to violate the NFZ treaty, and not to use or threaten to use nuclear weapons against any treaty party, or in the territory of any party to the treaty or to Protocol 1. Protocol 3 prohibited the testing of any nuclear device anywhere in the region. The 1985 Forum meeting had adopted the protocols in draft form. Subsequently, a representative delegation visited all five NWS capitals between January 28 and February 14, 1986, and then revised the protocols to give each party the right to withdraw from each protocol, upon a three-month notice, "if it decides that extraordinary events, related to the subject matter of the Protocol, have jeopardized its supreme interests." The seventeenth Forum meeting in Suva completed work on the protocols on August 8, 1986, and decided to open them for signature on December 1, 1986.

Threats to regional stability will arise from attempts by the USSR to challenge Western ascendancy, or from policy initiatives by the United States which provoke Soviet retaliation. The most important security goal for Australia and New Zealand in the South Pacific has been the strategic denial of the region to the Soviet Union.[5] The absence of a Soviet military presence in the region has precluded a direct security threat from this quarter. But increased power projection capability has meant an indirect threat since the 1970s. Derivative security interests include maintaining secure lines of communication between the ANZUS partners as a fallback should South China Sea, Indonesian archipelagic, and Malacca Strait lines be interdicted, and a denial of the same fallback lines to Soviet communication by a mix of successful sea assertion north of the equator and effective interdictory capability in the South Pacific. The United States has also entered into treaties of friendship with Kiribati, Tuvalu, and the Cook Islands which preclude bases from being provided to third countries without prior American consultations, and require consultations should threats be perceived to the islands' security. According to a State Department official, the object of the treaties—negotiated under the Carter Administration but ratified in 1983 under Reagan—was to renounce weak and obsolete U.S. territorial claims more than to enter into fresh military relationships.[6]

Much has been made in recent years of the significant expansion of the Soviet Navy in the Pacific and its enhanced power projection capabilities as a result of developments in Danang and Cam Ranh Bay in Vietnam. While the situation clearly merits constant monitoring, it is no cause for alarm. The combat capability of the Soviet Navy in the Pacific is limited by several factors. The open-ocean effectiveness of Soviet naval forces is

---

[5] See Richard A. Herr, "The Soviet Union in the South Pacific," in Ramesh Thakur and Carlyle A. Thayer, editors, *The Soviet Union as an Asian Pacific Power. Implications of Gorbachev's 1986 Vladivostok Initiative* (Boulder and Melbourne: West ew and Macmillan, 1987).

[6] John C. Dorrance, "United States Security Interests in the Pacific Islands," *Asia-Pacific Defense Forum* (Special Supplement, Winter 1985-1986), p. 8.

adversely affected by geographic constraints on their operations. The Western alliance is still regarded as having a favorable overall balance of maritime power in the Pacific, with advantages in such areas as amphibious assault forces, antisubmarine warfare, and sound quieting and detection capabilities. When to this are added the irrelevance of the Soviet economic model for the countries of the South Pacific, and the strong suspicions in the region of Soviet motives, it becomes clear that the Soviet Union lacks the ability, at least at present, to translate global military power into political and economic influence in the South Pacific. Australian Foreign Minister Bill Hayden noted at an April 1988 press conference in Manila that, according to Western intelligence estimates, Soviet naval activity in the Pacific had been reduced by 50 percent over the past year. Moreover, the USSR had also been "punctilious" in restricting its South Pacific activities to commercial operations. Therefore, while not losing "a sense of vigilance," Australia had failed to see "any evidence of any surge let alone threat of Soviet activity."[7]

A longstanding advocate of nuclear-weapon free zones, the Soviet Union became the first nuclear power to sign the relevant SPNFZ protocols (2 and 3) on December 15, 1986. But its signature of the protocols was qualified: it declared its compliance with protocol 2 to be conditional on party states not committing an act of aggression in alliance with another nuclear power or, during such aggression, permitting transit or visiting rights to air or sea vessels of a nuclear power. Continuing to project a new benign image in the region, the Soviet Union ratified the protocols on April 21, 1988; while its signature in 1986 was qualified, its ratification was not. It did not take China long to indicate support for the Treaty of Rarotonga; the Chinese ambassador to Fiji signed protocols 2 and 3 in Suva on February 10, 1987. China's instruments of ratification for the two protocols were deposited on January 4, 1989.

The United States and France were expected to be the two problematical nuclear powers. The Americans have been less than enthusiastic supporters of a NWFZ for the South Pacific. SPNFZ carefully avoided impinging upon the substantial U.S. nuclear involvement in the region, and its geographical limits specifically excluded U.S. Micronesian territories. The U.S. seizure of the Micronesian islands during the Second World War, and the transfer from Japan to the United States of the administration of the islands after the war, brought new Pacific responsibilities to Washington. Nearly all the islands north of the equator from the Philippines to the West coast of the United States were, for the first time, under U.S. control. Prior to World War II, Japan had administered the islands of Micronesia under a League of Nations Mandate. In 1947, the United Nations Security Council created the Trust Territory of the Pacific Islands—comprising the four political entities of the Northern Mariana Islands, Palau (also known as

---
7 Text of press conference supplied to author by the Australian High Commission in Wellington; a Reuter report was published in brief in the *Otago Daily Times*, April 15, 1988.

Belau), the Federated States of Micronesia (Kosrae, Ponape, Truk, and Yap), and the Marshall Islands—and formally transferred the mandate to the United States. In the 1980s, all four entities have moved separately to a Commonwealth (Northern Marianas) or Free Association relationship under compact with the United States.

With nuclear proliferation not being an issue in the region, and with the Soviet profile barely visible, Washington did not see any of its major security goals being served by the Treaty of Rarotonga. It was reported in April 1986 that the United States had adopted a tough uncompromising stand toward the Treaty. Washington had apparently concluded that the Australian initiative had been meant as a sop to party activists rather than as a serious commitment to regional nuclear arms control; that SPNFZ would directly benefit Soviet global objectives to the detriment of U.S. interests; and that SPNFZ could create a serious precedent for the establishment of interlocking NWFZs which would impede the free movement of U.S. forces around the world.[8] The formal U.S. decision not to sign the Rarotonga protocols was announced on February 4, 1987. Yet the compatibility of SPNFZ with U.S. security interests was demonstrated with the approval, without objection, of a "sense of the Congress" resolution by the House of Representatives in October 1987. Noting that SPNFZ was fully consistent with ANZUS and with U.S. security interests in the South Pacific, that it satisfied established U.S. criteria for NWFZs, and that signature and ratification would be in the U.S. national interest, the resolution urged the President to reconsider his decision not to sign the protocols to the Treaty of Rarotonga.[9]

On October 31, 1989, the Foreign Affairs Subcommittee on Asian and Pacific Affairs of the House of Representatives approved a proposed concurrent Congressional resolution urging that the United States sign the protocols to the Treaty of Rarotonga. Stephen Solarz, chairman of the subcommittee, explained that the treaty had been formulated in a way that was consistent with U.S. policy objectives. Nothing in the treaty impinged on U.S. interests, for the United States had no intention of deploying or permanently storing nuclear weapons in the South Pacific, testing nuclear weapons there, or threatening the countries of the region with nuclear attack. The United States should endorse the treaty as a mark of respect for the opinion of the countries of the region, Solarz said, noting that they were all friendly with the United States. Republican Congressman Robert Lagomarsino remarked that his previous doubts about signing the treaty had dissipated with the improved international situation.[10]

---

[8] Geoff Kitney, "U.S. Gets Tough with Australia over Nuclear-Free Zone," *National Times*, April 25, 1986, p. 5.

[9] *Australian Foreign Affairs Record (AFAR)*, Vol. 59, August 1988, p. 303.

[10] The text of the resolution and accompanying amplifying remarks were supplied to the author by the U.S. Embassy in Wellington.

The 1989 resolution provided seven points of justification for a U.S. endorsement of the Treaty of Rarotonga:

- U.S. policy has been to support the establishment of effective NWFZs in regions of nonproliferation concern where such zones would enhance international stability and security.

- The United States has a sevenfold set of criteria for judging the effectiveness of proposed NWFZs, namely: the initiative must come from within the region; all important countries in the region must participate; adequate verification of compliance must be provided; existing security arrangements must not be disturbed to the detriment of regional and international security; the development or possession of any nuclear device for any purpose must be prohibited for all zonal countries; international legal air and sea rights must be respected; international legal rights of transit privileges, including port calls and overflights, of zonal parties must be respected.

- The United States has signed and ratified the Treaty of Tlatelolco establishing a NWFZ in Latin America.

- The United States is also a party to treaties which preclude nuclear weapons from Antarctica, the seabed, and outer space.

- In testimony before the Congress in June 1987, a representative of the U.S. Arms Control and Disarmament Agency had stated that, in pursuit of nonproliferation goals, the United States continued to support efforts to establish effective NWFZs in Africa, the Middle East, and South Asia.

- Support for any one NWFZ does not prejudge U.S. policy on other proposed NWFZs, each of which must be judged on individual merits in accordance with U.S. national interests.

- The protocols to the Treaty of Rarotonga do not conflict with the principle of "neither confirm nor deny" and do not prohibit any current or anticipated U.S. activities in the region.

For these reasons, Congress expressed the sense that signature and ratification of the protocols to the Treaty of Rarotonga would be in the national interest of the United States. We should note that the 1989 resolution, in urging that the United States should sign and ratify, was somewhat more forceful than the 1988 resolution, which had urged the administration to reconsider its decision not to sign the treaty.

On November 7, 1989, the House of Representatives, with support from Democrats and Republicans, urged President George Bush to sign and ratify the protocols to the Treaty of Rarotonga.[11] The resolution expressed the sense of Congress but did not become law.

---

[11] *Otago Daily Times*, November 9, 1989.

The United States does not in fact conduct nuclear tests, base or store nuclear weapons, or dump nuclear waste in the South Pacific—or intend to do so. But the United States does have distinctive security relationships with Micronesian states, as noted above. The fact that the Marshall Islands and the Federated States of Micronesia are now members of the South Pacific Forum means that they have become eligible to join SPNFZ. Membership in the Forum and in SPEC would bring mutual advantages to other Micronesian territories upon the termination of the UN trusteeship: Micronesia would be reinvigorated with fresh ideas and the experience of non-ideological regional decisionmaking processes; the region would benefit from increased strength of numbers and enhanced economies of scale in the sorts of activities performed by SPEC. Yet Micronesian membership in the South Pacific Forum cannot but complicate the issue of inclusion of Micronesia within the zonal boundaries of the Treaty of Rarotonga, and the implications of this for U.S. accession to the protocols.

Britain followed the U.S. example by stating, on March 21, 1987, that signing the SPNFZ protocols would not serve its national interests, although it would not in practice act contrary to their requirements, and would keep its formal position under review.[12] The deciding factor with Britain was undoubtedly its relations with its two NATO allies, France and the United States. The net result is that the communist countries have signed, and the Western powers have not: the political repercussions of this alignment may be felt in due course.

Nuclear Testing

The fact that the South Pacific is the only region where nuclear testing is carried out by an extra-regional nuclear power,[13] namely France, gives particular cogency to antinuclear sentiments. As Australian Defence Minister Kim Beazley conceded subsequently, SPNFZ was aimed primarily at France.[14] The subject of French nuclear testing in turn is tied inseparably to what many South Pacific residents perceive as Gallic visions of grandeur as a world power, in the sense that Mururoa is irrelevant to French regional military strategy: it can be explained only at the level of European or global military strategy.

Not only can France be said to be a Pacific power; it is in fact the most substantial power in the South Pacific. It has three groups of island territories—"Confetti of the Empire"—in the region: New Caledonia, comprising the main island and six outlying island groups; the Wallis and Futuna islands to the northeast of Fiji (occupied in 1886); and French

---

[12] *Canberra Times*, March 22, 1987.

[13] The United Kingdom, of course, carries out tests at American sites. But because this is a bilateral arrangement, it does not invalidate the assertion made here of the uniqueness of French testing in an external *region*.

[14] *New Zealand Times*, September 1, 1985.

Polynesia, comprising five groups of islands administered from Papeete (Tahiti having been occupied in 1842). Successive French governments have reaffirmed the commitment to the security of all French overseas territories. In addition, French policy since the Second World War has been characterized by a continuity of conviction that France is a global power which must maintain the capability to project its military forces to any part of the world. The final consideration with a bearing on France's attitude toward its overseas possessions is the EEZ (exclusive economic zone)-based potential for commercial exploitation.

France has traditionally been an "activist" in its foreign policy, prepared to assert claims, and willing to act in defense of such claims. It is neither reticent in articulating its rights against external opposition, nor reluctant to commit troops as needed to protect or advance its self-proclaimed rights. Its rapid deployment force is structured, trained, and configured primarily for a swift response to national emergencies; but it can also, as a secondary objective, be deployed in response to overseas contingencies. Thus, France has the will and the ability to deploy its forces in the Pacific. Furthermore, overseas territories in the South Pacific give France ready bases for deploying force in the region. The two French overseas military commands in the Pacific are centered on New Caledonia and French Polynesia.[15] Given the tranquility of the region until very recently, French military forces, based at Papeete and Hao Island, have concentrated on the tasks of civil aid projects, training, EEZ maritime surveillance, and infrastructural support for nuclear tests. The naval repair facility in Tahiti is virtually self-sufficient in providing the necessary maintenance for the entire French Pacific fleet.

France can therefore be described as having the political will, the military muscle, and the infrastructural support facilities to project substantial power into the South Pacific. These general comments on French policy in the Pacific acquire particular cogency with regard to nuclear testing. France tests nuclear weapons in the South Pacific as a consequence of having decided to protect its status as a world power and to pursue the option of an independent nuclear deterrent. The decision on the independent deterrent was taken in the mid-fifties, with the Sahara being chosen as the initial testing site (1960-1963). France was compelled to relocate the testing site in 1963 after newly-independent Algeria objected to such activities in the Sahara; it was then shifted to the South Pacific. The tests embrace the variety of weapons systems constituting France's independent *force de frappe* (strike force). The French attitude seems to be that the bomb and the territory are French, the testing is done by France, so the choice of a testing site is solely a French decision. In September 1985, a spokesman for the French President took this argument a step

---

[15]See *The Military Balance 1987-1988* (London: International Institute for Strategic Studies, 1987), pp. 63-64.

further by declaring, while in Mururoa, that no country could take decisions in France's place with regard to its Pacific interests unless it wanted to be seen as an adversary.[16]

Countries of the South Pacific have been united, vocal, and persistent in their opposition to French nuclear testing. The opposition has been expressed by national leaders, through regional agencies, and in international forums. Nor is the opposition always confined to nice diplomatic language. For example, Senator Gareth Evans, representing the Minister for Foreign Affairs, was quite blunt in his statement in the Australian Parliament on September 12, 1985: "It is the Government's position that if France is as genuine as it claims to be in its assertions that no damage in terms of radioactive pollution will follow from the carrying out of those tests, it ought to put its money where its mouth is and conduct those tests on metropolitan French soil." The regional position is very simple and very clear. If the tests are harmful, they should be terminated; if they cause no harm, they should be conducted on metropolitan French soil.

The political fallout from the sinking of the *Rainbow Warrior* in 1985 focused international attention on French nuclear testing in the region.[17] The fact that the French testing brought the first act of international terrorism to New Zealand also strengthened regional opposition to French nuclear activities. Even after the international embarrassment of the *Rainbow Warrior* affair, nevertheless, France refused to budge on the issue of nuclear testing at Mururoa. Indeed, President François Mitterrand flew to Mururoa in mid-September 1985 to emphasize French determination on the subject, an act that was interpreted—and probably intended—as a calculated rebuff to pressure from the South Pacific countries to cease testing in the region.

Mitterrand's trip to Mururoa was chided as "an extremely provocative act" by Australian Foreign Minister Bill Hayden in Parliament on September 11. (This was still not as provocative as the returning of the two convicted agents to France in 1988, contrary to the terms of the UN Secretary-General's arbitration.) Hayden described the French motive as being "to evidence a tough determination to proceed with nuclear testing in the South Pacific." Subsequently, in a news release on October 25, Hayden repeated that if "France insisted on conducting these tests it should do so on its home territory, especially if the tests were as harmless as France claimed." He took issue with French claims that the report by scientists from Australia, New Zealand, and Papua New Guinea who visited Mururoa in 1983 established that the nuclear tests were completely harmless. The group had not cleared the tests in respect of long-term environmental

---

[16]Senator Gareth Evans in the Australian Parliament on September 16, 1985; *AFAR*, Vol. 56, September 1985, p. 872.

[17]See Ramesh Thakur, "A Dispute of Many Colours: France, New Zealand and the 'Rainbow Warrior' Affair," *World Today*, Vol. 42, December 1986.

consequences. And the South Pacific countries, unlike France, had no option but to be in the region for the long term. Therefore, Hayden concluded, "the presence of French political leaders at Mururoa Atoll could not legitimize France's nuclear testing program there."[18] (The French do not take kindly to the argument that Australia and New Zealand have the right to protest against the testing program at Mururoa because it is in their "backyard." Mururoa, they point out, is 7,100 km from Canberra; Semipalatinsk, the center for Soviet nuclear tests, is 5,200 km from Paris, and Bogota, Colombia is 4,500 km from the Nevada test site. Alice Springs, in the center of the Australian continent, is closer to the Chinese tests site of Lob Nor than to Mururoa.[19] The other nuclear powers' testing centers are much closer to major population centers than Mururoa; for example, the Nevada range is only 120 km from Las Vegas.)

More recently, a report tabled by the European Parliament's committee on the environment, public health, and consumer protection also noted "serious flaws" in the work and findings of the team of scientists from Australia, New Zealand, and Papua New Guinea which traveled to Tahiti and Mururoa Atoll in October 1983, headed by New Zealand National Radiation Laboratory Director Hugh Atkinson.[20] The Atkinson mission lacked medically qualified staff; it was barred from an independent choice of sampling sites on Mururoa; and it was not permitted to collect sediment from the lagoon. (On the other hand, France claims that it is the only nuclear power to have gone so far in cooperating with neighboring countries to establish relevant scientific data. Speaking to the UN General Assembly on September 28, 1983, President Mitterrand invited the other NWS to follow suit in respect of their testing ranges.) The committee, citing the number of studies which document the health effects of U.S. atmospheric nuclear tests in the Marshall Islands, called for the EC to pay for an independent team of scientists to investigate the health and environmental effects of French nuclear testing in the region; for the mission to have unrestricted freedom of investigation from French and Tahitian authorities; and for the World Health Organization to receive complete statistics on mortality rates and causes. More recently, a team led by underwater explorer Jacques Cousteau concluded that testing had produced deep fissures in Mururoa but no dangerous radioactivity. However, the team was not given sufficient geological information to be able to assess the

---

[18] *AFAR*, Vol. 56, October 1985, pp. 1046-1047.

[19] *French Nuclear Tests in Mururoa: The Reasons Why?* (Paris: Press Information Service of the Ministry of Foreign Affairs, n.d.), pp. 8-9.

[20] See David Robie, "Pressure Mounts for French Test Probe," *Dominion Sunday Times* (Wellington), June 19, 1988. The 1984 South Pacific Forum communique had noted that, although the Atkinson mission's findings "allayed to some degree the concern that had been expressed about the short-term effects of the French nuclear tests, they provided no reassurance about long-term consequences nor in any sense diminished Forum opposition to testing in any environment."

risks of serious radiation seepage through the volcanic rock to the sea or the surface over a period of time.[21]

There was a time-lag of nine years between the first atmospheric test and the first underground test at Mururoa in 1966 and 1975, respectively. The site was originally chosen because its isolation allegedly made it particularly suitable for atmospheric tests. The infrastructure built up after 1966 made Mururoa a *convenient* but not an *essential* site for underground testing; conversely, the economic and political costs of relocating could prove to be a substantial deterrent. (Foreign Minister Bill Hayden has pointed out that a technical report by Australia's own Office of National Assessments had concluded that France could safely carry out nuclear testing on the Massif Central of mainland France and in Corsica.)[22] Nor is the strategic justification for the program of nuclear testing self-evident. The case for a comprehensive test ban has not been disproved even worldwide; for France, *sufficiency* rather than over-ambitious parity seems adequate to its posture of deterrence. Sufficiency is quite compatible with maintaining the existing level of sophistication of nuclear weaponry and with the cessation of further testing. These two comments—on Mururoa as a convenient testing site and on the adequacy of sufficiency for the French strategic posture—are in addition to possible safety and environmental apprehensions, as well as harmful social, cultural, and political consequences in the region.

In September 1985, Prime Minister Hawke had approached the United States to exert pressure on France to cease nuclear testing in the Pacific. The Reagan Administration, however, confirmed the primacy of the North Atlantic over the South Pacific in its strategic worldview. The State Department described French nuclear tests as "essential to the modernization of the French nuclear deterrent"; in any case, the United States regarded "these matters as French decisions."[23] While the people who have to live in the South Pacific can understand U.S. concerns about the intricacies of an alliance which has been central to the defense of Europe, they also believe that such concerns belong to Europe. It is gratuitously offensive to subordinate Pacific sensitivities to European and global strategic calculations. The Australian Ambassador to the United States, F. Rawdon Dalrymple, used justifiably forceful language in an address to the Asia Society in Washington, D.C., on September 24, 1985: "If you want the South Pacific to become an area where the Soviet Union, Cuba and others of that stripe can find fertile ground for anti-United States, anti-West propaganda and activity and in which they can develop activities directly

---

[21] *Otago Daily Times*, November 12, 1988. The Cousteau team carried out a five-day investigation at the Mururoa site in June 1987.

[22] *AFAR*, Vol. 56, September 1985, pp. 865-866.

[23] Quoted by Denis Reinhardt, "Soviet Pledge on Nuclear-Free Zone Hits U.S. Diplomacy," *The Bulletin* (Sydney), April 1, 1986, p. 85.

prejudicial to our interest—then continue with a policy of indifference to what the French are doing there."[24]

French opposition to the South Pacific nuclear free zone is expressed on three counts: the major part of the zone comprises international seaspace free of any constraints; risks of horizontal proliferation are minimal in the South Pacific; the five nuclear-weapon states have already given negative security guarantees at an international level.[25] Given such an attitude on the part of the French government, it would appear unrealistic to expect a modification of its nuclear activity in the foreseeable future. In February 1987, France formally informed the South Pacific Forum that it would not adhere to any of the SPNFZ protocols. Its testing program at Mururoa continues unabated. The South Pacific countries simply lack the military, diplomatic, or economic clout to compel France to terminate its testing program. Such a conclusion is unlikely to stop regional countries from trying to change French policy, since in the long term the basis of opposition to French testing is more durable. As an Assistant Secretary in the New Zealand Ministry of Foreign Affairs noted, "No one pretends for a moment that [SPNFZ] will stop France testing, but it will serve further to isolate the French if they persist with this activity in face of the region's concern."[26]

Nuclear Infrastructure

France is unhappy with SPNFZ because it seeks to restrict French nuclear activity in the region. Yet the regime has not escaped criticism even from antinuclear groups. Activities of most concern to such groups—port calls, transit facilities for nuclear-capable aircraft, command, control, communications, and intelligence (C^3I) facilities in Australia and New Zealand, movement of nuclear-capable warships in the South Pacific waterways— remain untouched by the treaty.[27] The years since 1984 have seen a divergence even between Australia and New Zealand—the two white brothers of the South Pacific—on the most appropriate strategy of reducing the conflict potential and enhancing the security environment of their nations and region in the nuclear age. Australia is firm in its belief that it is part of the Western community of nations, and that an effective strategic balance under U.S. leadership is therefore in its national security interests.

---

[24]"Partners, Friends and Allies," *AFAR*, Vol. 56, September 1985, p. 823.

[25]"South Pacific Nuclear-Free Zone," in *France: Facts and Figures* (Wellington: Embassy of France, June 1985).

[26]Graham Fortune, "The South Pacific and New Zealand," *Perspectives of New Zealand's Foreign Policy* (Wellington: MFA Information Bulletin No. 18, 1986), pp. 29-30.

[27]In a written reply in Parliament on September 15, 1987, the Australian Defence Minister confirmed that British, French, Soviet, and U.S. nuclear-propelled and nuclear-capable warships had operated in the SPNFZ area since August 1986.

Conversely, a redistribution of power in favor of the Soviet Union globally, or an extension of Soviet influence regionally, would have an adverse impact upon Australian security interests and a destabilizing effect in the South Pacific region. Describing Australia as "a respected and self-respecting member of the Western community," the 1987 White Paper on defense set the goal of defense self-reliance "firmly within the framework of our alliances and regional associations. The support they give us makes self-reliance achievable."[28] The Australian paper specifically mentioned port visits by U.S. warships as an example of the opportunities provided to the Australian forces for combined exercises with advanced technology vessels, as well as providing rest and recreation facilities for U.S. naval deployments in the region. Australia's collective defense arrangements were viewed as enhancing self-reliance by improving technological capabilities, providing training opportunities for the armed forces, and facilitating access to vital military and political intelligence on both global and regional developments. Australia's access to the highest level of technology was explicitly described as "one of the most important benefits of our alliance with the United States."[29] As a practical example, the paper pointed out that the Jindalee OTHR (over-the-horizon radar) system was produced by Australian scientists building on access to U.S. technology. In return, the United States gains information from Australian surveillance and intelligence gathering activities.

A fundamental threat to Australian security would activate the ANZUS security guarantee. This guarantee also complicates the planning environment of a potential aggressor by making him contemplate the prospect of an allied response to an attack on Australia. But it is prudent for Australian defense planners to assume that the threshold of U.S. intervention could be quite high, and therefore to pursue policies of enhanced self-reliance to cope independently with a range of lower-level but more probable threats.

The Australian White Paper recognized that Australian security, like that of all other countries, is ultimately dependent upon a stable relationship between the two superpowers and the avoidance of nuclear war between them. Australia therefore believes that it is important to maintain a stable strategic balance to support mutual deterrence. As part of that process, Australia hosts joint defense facilities: the North West Cape Naval Communication Station in Western Australia, Pine Gap, and Nurrungar. The government of Australia accepted that the basing of joint facilities carried an attendant risk of Australia itself being a target in the event of nuclear conflict, but believed that the net damage to Australian security would be greater if the international strategic environment were to

---

[28]*The Defence of Australia* (Canberra: Australian Government Publishing Service, 1987), p. vii.

[29]Ibid., p. x.

deteriorate because of their dismantling. Subsequently, in a speech to the RAAF Staff College in May 1988, the Secretary of Foreign Affairs and Trade, Dr. Stuart Harris, remarked that Australia's willingness to host the joint facilities, accept ship visits, and help with B52 flights entitled and obliged it to a voice on global and regional arms control and disarmament policies.[30]

New Zealand has rocked the Western alliance boat rather vigorously in the last few years. The anti-ANZUS constituency blamed the military link with the United States for making New Zealand a nuclear target, compromising New Zealand's sovereignty, linking New Zealand to objectionable U.S. foreign policies, failing to guarantee New Zealand's security, and hindering the development of an indigenous threat-definition and intelligence-gathering capability. Major threats to New Zealand, its spokesmen argued, were difficult to discern, and the value of ANZUS was questionable against the more probable low-level threats.[31] While some did see value in ANZUS, they were not prepared to stay in the alliance at the cost of abandoning the antinuclear ships policy. The 1987 White Paper reiterated the commitment to ANZUS obligations, but "in conventional terms" only.[32]

The rationale for New Zealand's antinuclear posture, missing in the White Paper on Defence, was expressed by Prime Minister David Lange in an address to the Dunedin branch of the New Zealand Institute of International Affairs on April 30, 1987.

. . .nuclear weapons are themselves the greatest threat which exists to our future . . . far from adding to our security, they only put us more at risk. . . .

New Zealand cannot be defended by nuclear weapons and does not wish to be defended by nuclear weapons. We have disengaged ourselves from any nuclear strategy for the defence of New Zealand.

There would probably be general support for the claim made in a submission to the defense inquiry in 1986 that "The effects of New Zealand's nuclear warship ban is more significant than anything this country has ever done to try to promote international peace."[33] (This is not necessarily a creditable reflection on New Zealand's efforts in the field of international disarmament: gesture diplomacy cannot adequately substitute for a sub-

[30] *AFAR*, Vol. 59, May 1988, p. 183.

[31] For a description and discussion of the ANZUS alliance and the surrounding debate, see Ramesh Thakur, *In Defence of New Zealand: Foreign Policy Choices in the Nuclear Age* (Boulder, CO: Westview, 1986), chs.3 and 4.

[32] *Defence of New Zealand: Review of Defence Policy 1987* (Wellington: Government Printer, 1987), p. 31. For an analysis of the paper, see Ramesh Thakur, "New Zealand Defence Review 1985-1987," *Asian Defence Journal*, July 1987. For a comparison of the Australian, Canadian, and New Zealand defense white papers of 1987, see Ramesh Thakur, "God Defend the Queen: Three Commonwealth Defence White Papers," *Journal of Defense & Diplomacy*, Vol. 6, February 1988.

[33] *Defence and Security: What New Zealanders Want—Report of the Defence Committee of Enquiry, July 1986* (Wellington: Government Printer, 1986), p. 45.

stantive record.) New Zealand does believe that deterrence is divisible, and indeed that it is irrelevant to the security of New Zealand and the South Pacific region. As Lange explained in his April 1987 address:

When I think of the world's nuclear arsenals I know that what New Zealand has done as a measure of arms control [excluding nuclear warships from its ports] is a small step indeed. I also know that if we cannot take that step in New Zealand we cannot take it anywhere. If we cannot start in New Zealand we cannot start anywhere.

In short, while Australia supports ANZUS and hosts joint facilities by pointing to their conflict dampening role, New Zealand has distanced itself from aspects of the alliance because of perceptions of their conflict-generating potential. Furthermore, any attempt to bring a U.S. warship into a New Zealand port in the present socio-political environment would seriously split the country and lead to major confrontations on the streets. Given the marginal contribution of ship visits to the country's security, this would be a somewhat peculiar policy of national defense.

In addition to the joint facilities in Australia, the United States operates others in its Micronesian territories. U.S. nuclear testing in Micronesia ceased in 1962. Nevertheless, Kwajalein Atoll in the Marshall Islands has a permanent U.S. missile range (testing) facility; Guam has a nuclear stockpiling site and a strategic bomber base at Andersen airfield; both have C^3I facilities; and the United States has plans for establishing nuclear naval and air bases in Palau and the Mariana Islands. The Compact of Free Association between the United States and the three entities of the Marshall Islands, Palau, and the Federated States of Micronesia (FSM), because it has no exact precedent in international practice, has generated some confusion about U.S. motives and Micronesian independence of U.S. strategic calculations. The compact provides that the United States will defend the three states as it would the United States for a minimum period of 15 years in the cases of the Marshall Islands and the FSM, and 50 years in the case of Palau; has the right to preclude the military use of the territory of any of the three states by any third party; has the further right, in the case of Palau, under a Military Use and Operating Rights Agreement, to use various areas under certain contingencies and after consultation with the government of Palau;[34] and will have continued peacetime use of the Kwajalein missile range facility for 30 years.

Palau, which was placed under the supervision of the UN Security Council in 1947 (rather than the usual General Assembly supervision) by being designated a strategic trust, presented problems. The complicating element in its case came from Palau's constitutional requirement of a 75

---

[34]The 50-year agreement provides for contingency access to anchorage rights in Palau's main harbor and use of 40 acres of nearby land for support facilities; contingency joint use of the two main airfields; contingency use of 2,000 acres of land for logistics installations; and periodic access to Babelthuap Island for training exercises.

percent majority in a referendum on a compact. Such majority having proved unobtainable before—and the island's Supreme Court having upheld the constitutional ban against presidential attempts to circumvent it with the help of simple majority referendums—on August 4, 1987, a referendum amended the constitution to enable a compact to be approved by a simple rather than a three-quarter majority. Then, on August 21, 1987, a UN-observed plebiscite approved the Compact of Free Association by a 73 percent majority. Nevertheless, a three-quarter majority is still required to approve the use, testing, storage, or disposal of harmful substances, including nuclear weapons and waste. Under the compact, the United States may not engage in such proscribed activity but has the right to operate nuclear-capable and nuclear-propelled ships and aircraft within its global "neither confirm nor deny" policy. Suspicions remained that the United States was able to bribe its way out of a constitutional difficulty with a billion dollar aid package for 50 years—or US $1,230 per capita in Palau. In any event, in late August 1988 the country's Supreme Court again invalidated the two plebiscites of August 1987 and thereby frustrated the government's attempt to circumvent the antinuclear constitution.[35]

In light of these "loopholes" for the presence and entry of nuclear weapons into the South Pacific (SPNFZ permits nuclear ships to pass through zonal countries in transit or for rest and recreation), SPNFZ has been described as a "sham" by various opponents. One peace activist concluded that SPNFZ "seems more a cosmetic measure aimed at containing and defusing growing popular pressure for regional denuclearization than a serious move towards regional disarmament."[36] Furthermore, because the loopholes are largely in the categories of growing regional nuclearization, while the achievements lie in the marginal categories in the South Pacific, there is suspicion that SPNFZ may represent a net liability in serving to demobilize regional efforts at genuine denuclearization. As one critic put it, SPNFZ "permits and implicitly legitimizes the worst aspects of the nuclear arms race and superpower rivalry in the region."[37] For these reasons, the Treaty of Rarotonga has been ridiculed as an agreement by non-nuclear states to stay non-nuclear, akin to a "smoke-free zone" which applies only to nonsmokers.

The last comment in particular highlights the unfairness of the criticisms. A "smoke-free zone" is fully effective when smokers refrain from lighting up within the zone; they are not required to quit smoking permanently, nor even to hand over all cigarettes and matches to guardians of the zone at its gates. Similarly, a NWFZ will have achieved its objective if the nuclear-

---

[35] *Otago Daily Times*, September 1, 1988. See also Larry N. Gerston, "Palau: Trouble in Paradise," *New Zealand International Review*, Vol. 13, November/December 1988.

[36] Michael Hamel-Green, "South Pacific: A Not-So-Nuclear-Free Zone," *Peace Studies*, October 1985, p. 6.

[37] Ibid., November/December 1985, p. 42. The article was published in two parts.

weapons states refrain from lighting up their nuclear arsenals within the zone. Attempts to ban transit of nuclear-armed ships through zonal high seas, by being legally impermissible and practically unenforceable, would merely generate international skepticism toward the zone as a whole. The framers of the treaty were guided by the principle of "stretching the fabric of the Treaty to its widest possible extent."[38] Some of the attacks on SPNFZ arise from a confusion between an arms control and a confidence building measure (CBM). SPNFZ is defective if viewed as an arms control agreement. Yet it remains valuable as a CBM which enlarges and deepens the area of peace. It does not eliminate the possibility of nuclear weapons use in the South Pacific; it does promote security and raise the threshold of nuclear initiation in the region by reducing instabilities, and diminishing uncertainties about military arrangements by facilitating exchanges of information on nuclear-related military activity. SPNFZ is primarily a means of influencing the nature of peacetime relations between the nuclear-weapon states in the South Pacific.

Environment

In the distinctive marine environment of the South Pacific, the ocean is viewed by islanders both as a primary source of food and as a means of bringing vastly separated peoples together: hence, finally, the peculiar significance of the seas to the Pacific peoples and their sharpened anxieties about possible ecological degradation.

The Treaty of Rarotonga went beyond the minimalist definition of NWFZs. First, the title itself was of some significance. A nuclear weapons free zone suggests an arms control objective. Indications that the Japanese intended to dump low-level radioactive waste in the North Pacific in the 1970s, and again in 1982, sensitized the peoples of the Pacific to the issue of toxic waste disposal; SPNFZ prohibited the dumping of any nuclear waste in the zone (Article 7). The treaty also called for parties to support the conclusion of a global convention on the matter. After four years of negotiations, a convention for the protection and development of the region's natural resources and environment, the South Pacific Regional Environmental Programme (SPREP), was adopted at a plenipotentiary conference of the South Pacific Commission member governments in Noumea on November 25, 1986. The convention area comprises the EEZs of all Pacific island countries and territories, and also those areas of the high seas which are enclosed from all sides by Pacific EEZs. The convention is concerned with the protection of the marine environment against pollution from land-based sources, seabed activities, and storage of toxic and hazardous wastes; the prohibition on dumping of radioactive waste

---

[38]David Sadleir, "Rarotonga: In the Footsteps of Tlatelolco," *AFAR*, Vol. 58, September/ October 1987, p. 492. Sadleir was Chairman of the Working Group of Officials on SPNFZ appointed by the South Pacific Forum in 1984 to produce a draft treaty for the 1985 Forum meeting.

applies irrespective of whether or not such dumping causes pollution. The convention obliges parties to "prevent, reduce and control" pollution from any source; sets up a blacklist of substances that cannot be put into the ocean under any circumstances, e.g.., mercury, oil, and certain plastics; and requires special permission for dumping some other substances, e.g., arsenic, lead, and nickel. While nuclear testing is not prohibited, parties are committed to sound environmental management in regard to the consequences of nuclear testing. The prohibition of any future dumping constituted a significant concession by France and the United States, both of which signed the convention on November 25, 1986. SPREP thus constitutes a significant international regime for the protection of the marine environment of the region. (Some of the island countries of the region face particularly grave environmental threats from the so-called greenhouse effect. At a meeting of experts convened in Yugoslavia by the United Nations Environmental Programme, it was stated that Kiribati, the Line Islands, the Marshall Islands, Tokelau, and Tuvalu face extinction with moderate rather than extreme projection scenarios of rising sea levels.)[39]

Conclusions

It would be useful at this point to recapitulate the six strands of regional nuclear concerns and to anticipate briefly their future developments. It was argued that the authority of the superpowers as defenders of the world order has been eroding somewhat in recent times because they have been perceived by much of the world community as failing to discharge their duty responsibly. Soviet-American dialogue and agreements in the 1960s and 1970s built up a structure of cooperation which embodied the world's hopes for an avoidance of nuclear war. As the process of detente ground to a halt by the end of the 1970s and suffered reverses in the first half of the 1980s, the fruits of earlier cooperation began to decay and the two superpowers abandoned their postures as responsible managers of the world order. As the superpowers re-established a structure of confrontation, they lost virtually all claim to be regarded as the nuclear trustees for mankind: the circle of countries that still regarded them as the "great responsibles" was a steadily diminishing one in the early 1980s.[40] The advent of Gorbachev in the USSR and policies adopted during the second term of the Reagan Administration have produced dramatic improvements in the international atmospherics between the superpowers. It does not seem unreasonable to suggest that alarmist anxieties about an outbreak of nuclear war have been correspondingly dampened. To that extent, the global nuclear anxieties of South Pacific peoples have been partially assuaged. How durable this is remains to be seen.

---

[39] Geoffrey Lean, "Island Nations that are Under Threat," *Otago Daily Times*, October 29, 1988, utilizing the London Observer Service.

[40] See Hedley Bull, "The Great Irresponsibles? The United States, the Soviet Union, and World Order," *International Journal*, Vol. 25, Summer 1980.

As for superpower rivalry in the South Pacific, the region has long been regarded as a Western lake, and owes a substantial part of its history of freedom from cold-war tensions and crises to this fact. Western ascendancy has been achieved alongside a low-profile U.S. military presence, with no U.S. ships, aircraft, or forces being based in the South Pacific. Military technological advances have also rendered the island stepping-stones strategy of World War II obsolete in modern times. Nor has Washington been required to assume an internal security role outside its own territorial responsibilities. It has been happy to accept broader Western security interests in the South Pacific coming under Australian-New Zealand jurisdiction with correspondingly diminished political costs for island countries. After the Washington-Wellington rift in the ANZUS alliance,[41] and in the wake of intensified anxieties about stability in the region following coups in Fiji and outbreaks of violence in New Caledonia and Vanuatu, Australia has moved toward strengthening its own surveillance, monitoring, and demonstration activities.

The de facto nuclear free status of the South Pacific was formalized in the Treaty of Rarotonga. The goals behind the establishment of SPNFZ were the need to prevent the region from becoming a theater of superpower rivalry; the need to preserve in perpetuity the existing peace and security of the region; and the wish to protect the natural resources on which the well-being and livelihood of the South Pacific peoples depend. Regional disarmament can at best supplement universal disarmament. Efforts toward the first are spurred by lack of visible progress in the latter. Because the effects of nuclear war would be global and species-threatening, all countries have both the right and the responsibility to make efforts toward halting and then reversing the nuclear arms race. The hope is that each step forward, such as a nuclear-weapons-free zone, will lessen the suspicion and distrust that underlies the arms race. While comprehensive disarmament remains a long-range goal of the international community, the conviction has grown that immediate and partial measures which would increase confidence and create a more favorable atmosphere for overall disarmament should be pursued. Arms control efforts look too much to the past, and are reactive and curative. For a region that seeks to perpetuate the status quo of isolation from nuclear weapons strategy and deployment, the greater need is for measures that are anticipatory and preventive. The SPNFZ can be commended for being prophylactic rather than abortive or therapeutic. This therefore gives it a military significance additional to its political importance as a means of raising the threshold of nuclear initiation and as a confidence building measure.

There is a rough consensus in the South Pacific that the Treaty of Rarotonga is a practical confidence building measure. Yet even during the negotiation of SPNFZ, differences emerged over how strict the antinuclear regime

---

[41] For a fuller discussion of the New Zealand-U.S. dispute, see Thakur, *In Defence of New Zealand*, op. cit., ch. 8.

should be. The Melanesians in particular would have preferred to tighten some of the apparent loopholes. Papua New Guinea and Vanuatu tried unsuccessfully to define stationing in a way that would place limits on the frequency and duration of nuclear ship visits. As it stands, the distinction between formal basing, prohibited by SPNFZ, and de facto home-porting, permitted by SPNFZ, can be easily blurred in practice. Indeed, Cockburn Sound in Western Australia is host to nuclear submarines approximately 25 percent of the time. Nauru, Papua New Guinea, the Solomon Islands, and Vanuatu tried unsuccessfully to extend Protocol 3 of SPNFZ so as to prohibit the testing of missiles as well as warheads. And Nauru and Vanuatu were no more successful in seeking to ban uranium exports by parties to SPNFZ; in fact, Australia subsequently resumed uranium sales to France, an action which eroded the credibility of its anti-testing stance in the region.

A Fiji Anti-Nuclear Group (FANG) campaigned to give more teeth to SPNFZ as well, and held an "alternative forum" in Suva in August 1986. The elections of April 1987 saw the defeat of the 17-year old Alliance Government headed by Ratu Sir Kamisese Mara. The new Fijian government of Dr. Timoci Bavadra had promised to emulate New Zealand's nuclear-free policies; Mara by contrast had a reputation as an instinctive friend of the West. In an interview with an Australian political scientist in 1986, Bavadra accepted that both the United States and the Soviet Union were superpowers, and said that a Labour Government would strive for a balanced relationship with the two, while looking to New Zealand on nuclear issues.[42] Indications of a nonaligned policy by his government after the 1987 election threatened to undermine Western strategic-political interests in the South Pacific region, and this was but one of several reasons for the coup of May 1987 advanced by Colonel Sitiveni Rabuka.[43]

Yet the issue of visits by nuclear-propelled and nuclear-armed ships to countries of the South Pacific is likely to remain contentious in the foreseeable future. Even Australian public opinion has undergone important shifts on this. Support for the ANZUS alliance remains strong with two-thirds of Australians. But where 47 percent supported visits by nuclear-armed ships in 1982, with 44 percent opposed,[44] in September 1988 support had dwindled to 22 percent, and opposition had increased to 46 percent.[45] There was a problem too when the British aircraft carrier HMS Ark Royal

---

[42]Stephanie Hagan, "Race, Politics and the Coup in Fiji," Paper presented to the Australasian Political Studies Association conference, Auckland, 1987, pp. 27-28.

[43]For analyses of the coup, see Brij. V. Lal, Power and Prejudice: The Making of the Crisis in Fiji (Wellington: New Zealand Institute of International Affairs, 1988); and Ramesh Thakur and Antony Wood, "Paradise Regained or Paradise Defiled? Fiji under Military Rule," International Studies, Vol. 26, January-March 1989.

[44]Andrew Mack, "Gathering of the Doves," The Bulletin (Sydney), September 6, 1988, p. 63.

[45]Pacific Research (Canberra), November 1988, p. 26.

was forced to languish in heavy seas off Melbourne in October 1988 because shipping unions, alleging that the ship carried nuclear weapons, refused to help berth it.[46]

The nuclear paradox referred to above is a factor that helps to explain the opposition to infrastructural nuclear facilities sited in the region, even though they may play a role in assuring strategic stability. The damage that they might cause to the host nations as priority targets of retaliation during a nuclear exchange exceeds, in the opinions of some, any benefits that they might provide in delaying that eventuality. This has begun to shift Australian public attitudes. Where 60 percent supported the presence of U.S. communications bases on Australian soil in 1980,[47] the figure had dropped to 36 percent by September 1988.[48]

The subject of French testing too is likely to remain a troublesome issue in the South Pacific as far as one can see into the future, even though there is a clear consensus among all others that the testing should cease. France carried out its latest series of tests in French Polynesia in May-June 1989. The environmental consequences of the testing program are feared rather than proven, although a Canadian geographer, Gary Whiteford of the University of New Brunswick, was reported as suggesting a link between nuclear tests and earthquakes within one to three days.[49]

Australia supports efforts to maintain a stable strategic balance, and accepts the need for current levels of arsenals by the West "as a basis for substantive arms control and disarmament negotiations."[50] For Australia, the path to diminished international tension lies through verifiable arms control agreements in both nuclear and conventional fields. Australia and New Zealand are united nevertheless in their support of a comprehensive test ban (CTB)—which was endorsed by a record 146 nations in a United Nations General Assembly vote in December 1988, with only France and the United States voting against it—and are prepared to participate in the development and management of a global seismic monitoring network to verify compliance with a CTB. The two countries, which participate actively in the work of the Group of Scientific Experts, signed a seismic monitoring agreement on April 30, 1987. The GSE also designated Australia as one of four international data centers for the major network trial planned for 1988-1989. In September 1986 the Australian government opened the Australian Seismological Centre in Canberra whose purpose is to draw

---

[46] *Otago Daily Times*, October 15, 1988. For a discussion of ship visit policies of a number of countries around the world, see Robert E. White, *Nuclear Ship Visits: Policies and Data for 55 Countries* (Dunedin: Tarkwode Press, 1989).

[47] Mack, op. cit., p. 63.

[48] *Pacific Research*, November 1988, p. 26.

[49] *New Zealand Herald*, November 29, 1988.

[50] *Defence of Australia*, op. cit., p. 10.

together information from seismic stations and arrays in Australia and Antarctica; in June 1987 the government dedicated a new seismic array processor, capable of detecting and identifying nuclear explosions at the main Chinese, French, Soviet and U.S. test sites, which will provide enhanced analysis of seismic data.

Finally, the countries of the region are at one with extra-regional states in having solemnly accepted that no radioactive waste should be dumped in the South Pacific. Looking at SPNFZ and SPREP together, on this at least one can end on a happy note for the future.

ASEAN Relations with the South Pacific Island Nations

by Jusuf Wanandi

In the 1960s and 1970s the South Pacific region was very much a "lake" of the Western alliance. The U.S. presence in this part of the world was predominant. This derived generally from the strength of the Seventh Fleet in the Pacific and more specifically by virtue of the special relations of the United States with Micronesia, Palau, the Northern Mariana Islands, and the Marshall Islands, in the northern part of the South Pacific. However, the American presence in the entire region has been manifested since 1951 mainly through ANZUS, in which the regional powers, Australia and New Zealand, have been allied with the United States—although the alliance was fractured in 1985 by U.S.-New Zealand differences over nuclear policy.

The 1980s saw dramatic changes in the region. From the outside, these changes are often seen as seriously disturbing the tranquility of earth's last paradise. From the inside, however, many of the changes taking place are considered desirable and welcome. The political developments and social changes in many of these small island nations, as well as in Papua New Guinea, and the instabilities that sometimes accompany them, are perhaps a necessary part of their nation-building process. However, there is a growing concern on the part of many that the changing external environment could greatly complicate their developmental tasks, and that the instabilities in these countries could be exploited by external powers for their broader regional or global interests. Thus, from the perspective of the United States and much of the Western alliance, the Soviet Union's increased presence in the region, diplomatically, commercially, and perhaps also militarily, poses a serious threat to regional stability. There are other factors adding to this concern: for example, the adoption of the South Pacific Nuclear Free Zone (SPNFZ); the greater assertiveness on the part of South Pacific island countries to establish their rights over and to guard their Exclusive Economic Zones (EEZ); and the rift within ANZUS itself as a result of U.S. opposition to New Zealand's antinuclear policy.

The Soviet move into the South Pacific began in the early 1980s, but its interest in the region was not articulated until Gorbachev delivered his famous Vladivostok speech in 1986. Since then, the Soviet Union has pursued a policy toward the region based on the following five issues: (1) criticism of U.S. policies in Micronesia; (2) support for New Caledonia's independence; (3) support for the SPNFZ; (4) support for New Zealand's antinuclear policy; and (5) advancement of the Soviet concept and policy of "equal security."[1] Soviet approaches in the commercial field have met with only mixed results thus far: Its fishery agreement of 1985 with Kiribati was discontinued because of insufficient compensation, but it successfully negotiated a broader agreement in 1987 with Vanuatu, including on-land facilities and trans-shipment of the catch. There is a concern that Moscow's accumulation of information on the region's hydrography and topography and its military geography in general, including seabed and marine resources, might give it an edge in strategic-military terms.

The danger exists that the growing Soviet interest and presence in the South Pacific could extend the superpower conflict into the area, thus increasing pressures upon various countries in the region and upon the region as a whole. There is even some concern that a handful of the small island nations could lose their national sovereignty.[2] Washington's policy toward the region may prove to be crucial to its future.

In the near future, the Soviet military presence in the region is not likely to pose a real challenge to the United States. However, U.S. leaders will clearly face a changed environment from the previous one in which the American presence in this region went largely uncontested. Moreover, some parts of the ANZUS Treaty have become inoperative as a consequence of New Zealand's refusal to allow nuclear-powered and nuclear-weapons-carrying ships to visit its harbors. Some resentment toward the United States on the part of a number of the island countries has resulted from a lack of sensitivity on the part of the United States regarding the importance of EEZs to these countries. In fact, this discontent may have led some island nations to welcome Soviet approaches toward the region. The 1987 fisheries agreement between the United States and 13 South Pacific Forum (SPF) countries involving a compensation of $60 million over a period of five years appears to have defused the growing antagonism on this issue.

There is also the larger issue of the South Pacific Nuclear Free Zone. The United States has refused to sign the protocols of the Rarotonga Agreement that established the SPNFZ, partly because of its concern that this nuclear free zone would be emulated by other regions in the world and

---

[1] See David Hegarty, *South Pacific Security Issues: An Australian Perspective* (Canberra: The Strategic and Defence Studies Centre, Working Paper No. 147, December 1987). By "equal security" the Soviets originally meant that Moscow and Washington have equal access and presence in the South Pacific. Later, Soviet spokesmen clarified the statement by saying that it calls especially for a Soviet political presence in the region and economic cooperation between the Soviet Union and the South Pacific countries.

[2] Ibid.

partly to express solidarity with France. This stance has had a negative effect on U.S. standing and popularity in the region, especially because in contrast the Soviet Union belongs to the first set of countries that agreed to sign Protocol 2 of the agreement, by which nuclear powers can indicate their adherence to SPNFZ principles. Perhaps it is of less importance to the South Pacific countries that the Soviet Union attached a number of qualifications to its signing of the protocol.

In many of the South Pacific island countries, internal developments by now have reached a certain momentum and patterns of change have become fairly well established. In fact, some changes are rather dramatic and could have broad regional implications, including an impact on U.S. strategic interests in the region. Although U.S. policies toward the South Pacific should give proper attention to potential Soviet challenges, first priority should be assigned to a correct appreciation of the changing national aspirations of the new leaders and elites in those countries. A continuation of U.S. support for French nuclear testing in Mururoa, for example, would severely damage the American political image in the region.

A new generation is in the process of taking over leadership throughout the region. The national aspirations of these leaders differ from those of the older generation because they do not have the emotional attachment to the West of their predecessors. Therefore, their eagerness to develop close relations with the Western countries should not be taken for granted. Their concern with national development is real, but they also have a deep sense of vulnerability in view of the limited economic resources of their small island countries .

Continued cooperation with Australia and New Zealand is likely to be the first priority on the American agenda for the South Pacific, and such an approach would be supported by U.S. allies in the region.[3] In addition, another U.S. ally, Japan, has in recent years shown an increased interest in the region and a willingness to provide economic aid. Indeed, Japan is likely to become the most important source of future economic assistance to the region. No doubt the United States and Japan will coordinate their policies in providing development assistance to the South Pacific island countries. The ASEAN countries can also play an important role in this regard by virtue of their relevant development experiences and efforts which by and large have produced positive results. In the area of development cooperation, the ASEAN countries can make a significant contribution to stability in the South Pacific, but they can perhaps help most by developing sound political relations with the South Pacific island countries.

---

[3] As stated by The Hon. Kim C. Beazley, MP, Australian Minister of Defence in "Australia's Defence Policy," paper presented at the Bicentennial Conference on "Australia and the World: Prologue and Prospects," Canberra, December 6-9, 1988.

In the following two sections, we will examine a number of developmental and regional issues that could provide a basis for the strengthening of relations between ASEAN and the South Pacific.

National and Developmental Issues in the South Pacific

There are two main issues that will have a significant influence on the future development of the South Pacific region: economic development and leadership changes.[4]

One rather common economic feature of the small island nations is their narrow economic base and their heavy dependence upon external financial assistance. In recent years, most of these nations have experienced stagnant economic development. Apart from unfavorable trends in commodity prices, aid from traditional sources—Australia and New Zealand—has generally declined. In view of the modest amounts involved, Japan could easily provide the required capital. The main problem lies perhaps with the limited absorptive capacity of these narrowly based economies. It is clear that development assistance should seek to create a more diversified economic structure which would help to reduce their vulnerability. In addition, economic linkages with larger markets need to be created in order to increase the economic viability of these island nations.

Indeed, there is no shortage of ideas and recommendations for the strengthening of these economies. However, it is the various essential economic linkages to the industrialized countries and to the larger international markets and their unknown effects upon national sovereignty that cause these small countries to be anxious about their independence. It is not immediately clear how such anxieties might find expression in the foreign policies of these countries, but one possibility could well be efforts to counterbalance one external power against another.

The ASEAN countries, despite their much larger and stronger economies, have experienced the same anxieties in the past and therefore can understand them. The involvement of ASEAN in a triangular scheme of development cooperation between the industrialized countries and the South Pacific island nations has been proposed to take advantage of the fact that ASEAN's level of development is not too far ahead of that of the South Pacific countries, and the two groups face some important common economic problems. However, ASEAN's contribution to such a scheme would probably be mostly political in nature, namely in terms of political bridge-building and political partnership.

National economic development ranks as a major strategic issue for the region. Indeed, perhaps it is the most important, not only in view of the foreign policy implications of continued economic vulnerability, but also because stagnant economies would greatly complicate internal social and

---

[4] Hegarty, op. cit.

political developments, including frustrating the efforts of new leaders to improve the standard of living of their peoples.

Today, problems of unemployment, urbanization, crime, social unrest, as well as separatist movements are commonly faced by a number of countries in the South Pacific, largely as a result of worsening economic performance. Developments in Fiji are a case in point, albeit not entirely a representative one. The inability of the political system to deal effectively with the problem of changes in the economic situation of indigenous Fijians seems to have led to Sitiveni Rambuka's coups in May and September 1987. But the problems remain unresolved in 1990. Lee Kuan Yew of Singapore correctly points out that unless Fiji takes action to stimulate its economy and to improve the economic and educational status of indigenous Fijians in a fundamental way, a new constitution may not be sufficient to bring about social and political stability.[5]

The severe economic challenges faced by the countries in the region can also be seen in the case of Papua New Guinea, even though it is in a far more favorable situation than the other countries because of its sizeable natural resources. The development strategy adopted by the first Somare Cabinet (1974-1980), which was equity- rather than growth-oriented, turned out to be a failure. It resulted in severe unemployment among the youth and a sharp rise in crime rates. This led to the adoption of a growth-oriented development strategy during and after the second Somare Cabinet. The mining sector has become the main engine of growth, but the enclave nature of this sector suggests that efforts to diversify the economic structure must be undertaken. Failure of the present government's development efforts would most likely radicalize the internal situation and could have wide-ranging regional implications.

Kiribati's fishery agreement with the Soviet Union, involving insufficient compensation from Moscow, suggests the desperate situation in which some of these countries find themselves. Although political motivations played a role, Vanuatu's fishery agreement with the Soviet Union and its relations with Libya are also based on economic considerations.

The second national issue, namely that of generational change in leadership throughout the South Pacific, can be viewed from different perspectives. The region is witnessing the emergence of new leaders who are straying from the Westminster tradition and who desire to reduce overdependence on their traditional patrons, Australia and New Zealand. They are more nationalistic than the older generation, and their foreign policy agenda is to diversify relations and, in particular, to broaden relations with neighboring countries, namely the ASEAN states, as well as with the major powers, including the Soviet Union.

---

[5] Prime Minister Lee Kuan Yew's interview in *The Straits Times*, November 11, 1988, p. 1.

Papua New Guinea has been in the forefront of such diplomatic activities. It entered into a Treaty of Mutual Respect, Friendship and Cooperation with Indonesia in 1986 and a security cooperation agreement with Australia in 1987. In 1988, it became a signatory of ASEAN's Treaty of Amity and Cooperation. For many years, Papua New Guinea has been sending an observer to ASEAN Ministerial Meetings; indeed, it is the only regular observer, giving it a de facto special status. By its presence at these meetings, Papua New Guinea is widely regarded as representing the interests of the South Pacific region, specifically the South Pacific Forum (SPF).

A more recent diplomatic step taken by Papua New Guinea involves an agreement for the Soviet Union to open an embassy in Port Moresby, a move seen in PNG as a symbol of its desire to enter into a more balanced relationship with the great powers and of its independence to develop relations with any country it deems important. Papua New Guinea's more active role is also manifested in the leadership position it has assumed in the "Melanesian spearhead group" within the SPF, aimed at speeding up the process toward New Caledonia's independence.

Developments in Fiji during the past few years clearly show how internal political changes have affected the country's foreign policy. In fact, Rambuka is one of a number of figures representing a second generation of leaders, called *Takei*, whose main concern is with the role and position of indigenous Fijians in the economy and society. This group proposes that indigenous Fijians should be given certain privileges that are to be guaranteed by a new constitution. At the same time, there has been a reorientation of Fiji's foreign relations away from the traditional ties and relations with Great Britain, Australia, and New Zealand. The government in Suva has strengthened relations with the ASEAN countries and France. As suggested earlier, a new constitution alone may not solve the ethnic problem in view of the prevailing large gap between the indigenous Fijians and the Indian population in terms of entrepreneurial capabilities and other skills. Meanwhile, the economy remains stagnant, if not deteriorating, a factor that adds to the difficulty of solving already complex socio-political problems.

Vanuatu's internal political situation and its foreign policy stance are largely a product of its bloody struggle for independence only a few years ago. A new, younger leadership has not yet emerged in Vanuatu, and the shift within its first generation of leaders continues to affect not only the country's internal stability but also its foreign relations. Prime Minister Walter Lini has recently made approaches to Australia and New Zealand in the hope of receiving some support in countering Barak Sope, the General Secretary of the government party, Vanna'aku Pati, who is more radical and has promoted relations with Libya. Developments in New Caledonia, which will be examined later, will also have a significant influence upon trends in the region.

The changes mentioned above proceeded much faster in the Melanesian than in the Polynesian part of the region, but the time will come when the winds of change will blow throughout the entire region. The 1990s may see greater uncertainties in the development of the South Pacific. Regional states may adopt a much more nationalistic stance on internal and external matters; they may take a more neutral international posture and may continue to loosen ties with Australia, New Zealand, and the United States, and strengthen ties with other countries, including the Soviet Union, but they will refrain from moving toward alignment with Moscow.

Nonetheless, Australia and New Zealand, as members of the SPF, continue to play an important role in the broader regional issues of the South Pacific, such as the implementation of the SPNFZ and the decolonization of New Caledonia. These issues will be examined in the next section.

South Pacific Regional Issues

French policies in the South Pacific have a direct bearing on two of the most important regional issues: the decolonization of New Caledonia and the denuclearization of the region. The Socialist Government of President François Mitterrand and Premier Laurent Fabius began the decolonization process in 1985 through compromises that were acceptable to the indigenous people, the Kanaks, who comprise about 43 percent of the population of New Caledonia. The plan, known as "independence-in-association," as a step toward full independence, involved the granting of full autonomy to the four administrative regions, of which three would be under the authority of the Kanaks and the fourth one, namely Noumea, the capital city, would be under the administration of the French inhabitants.

With a change in the French government in early 1986, new Premier Jacques Chirac withdrew the plan and also put a halt to land reform. This was a setback for the Kanaks, while the influence of the French population in Noumea increased. The pressures in France itself to keep New Caledonia within the French Republic, especially among the conservatives who were Chirac's supporters, also increased. The Kanak Socialist National Liberation Front, the major group advocating independence for New Caledonia, urged the Kanaks to boycott the 1987 referendum on the future status of New Caledonia. Most did, but some 17 percent cast ballots. Official totals show that 58 percent of the total electorate voted, and that 98 percent of those voting supported retaining New Caledonia's ties to the French Republic. A proposal made in early 1988 for dividing the territory equally among the pro-independence group and the pro-France group was also unacceptable to the Kanaks. Their dissatisfaction led to an armed conflict at the time of the presidential elections in France in May 1988.

The return of a Socialist Government in France under President Mitterrand and Socialist Premier Michel Rocard opened up the possibility for new negotiations. This resulted in a treaty, known as the Matignon agreements, which provides for one year of direct rule from Paris and nine years of autonomy with local elections, to be followed by a referendum in New Caledonia on the question of independence. In a November 1988 referendum, 80 percent of the voters casting ballots in France approved the Matignon agreements; in New Caledonia itself, 57 percent backed the agreements. Thus, the plan has been implemented, and the ten-year transition period should help the Kanaks to prepare adequately for independence at the end of this century. Although the Kanak leader who helped forge the Matignon agreements, Jean-Marie Tjibaou, was assassinated in May 1989 by a radical separatist, the resulting crisis over the future of New Caledonia seems to have been overcome due to the statesmanship of Tjibaou's successor and followers. It is clearly in the region's interest that the transition to independence proceeds smoothly. If asked to provide assistance, ASEAN would definitely extend a helping hand by providing opportunities for training in such fields as public administration or management.

The desire for a denuclearized South Pacific, as expressed in the SPNFZ concept established by the Rarotonga Treaty, has deep psychological roots among the peoples of the island nations. They are concerned that the world simply regards their area as a testing ground without giving due regard to the fellow human beings who happen to live there. The region has been used for the testing of atomic and hydrogen bombs since World War II, most recently for nuclear testing by France. In the 1970s there also was talk that Japan might use the area for storing low-radiation nuclear waste. France's arguments that the testing is necessary for the maintenance of its independent nuclear strategy and capability, that French Polynesia is a French territory, and that its continued presence in the South Pacific contributes to regional stability are unacceptable to the peoples of the region, and their opposition is likely to mount in the future.[6]

The genesis of the Rarotonga Treaty can be found in the region's obvious concern with the health and survival of its people. The treaty was adopted at the 16th South Pacific Forum meeting in Rarotonga, Cook Islands, on August 6, 1985, and went into effect on December 11, 1986, when Australia became the eighth country to ratify the treaty. Prior to Australia, it had been ratified by Fiji and the Cook Islands (both in October 1985), Tuvalu (January 1986), Niue (May 1986), Western Samoa and Kiribati (both in October 1986), and New Zealand (November 1986). Nauru, the Solomon Islands, and Papua New Guinea followed Australia with their ratifications (April

---

[6] Ramesh Thakur, "The South Pacific Nuclear Free Zone," paper presented at the First Conference on "The Relationship between Indonesia and the South Pacific Countries," Hasanuddin University, December 6, 1988.

1987, January 1989, and September 1989, respectively). Tonga and Vanuatu have not yet signed the treaty.

Together with the nuclear free zones in Latin America (based on the Treaty of Tlatelolco of 1967, the first nuclear weapons free zone in an inhabited region) and in the Antarctic (the Antarctic Treaty of 1959, the first NWFZ in the world), these three zones cover about 40 percent of the earth's surface. The Rarotonga Treaty has a broader coverage than the Tlatelolco Treaty because it forbids nuclear waste storage. In addition, while the Rarotonga Treaty entered into force after ratification by eight countries out of the thirteen that drafted it, the Tlatelolco Treaty requires ratification by all eligible (Latin American) states, including ratification of both protocols— except that the treaty will enter into force for those parties that have waived the above requirements and have deposited their instruments of ratification. Moreover, under the latter treaty, a signatory may denounce the treaty after giving only a three-month notice on grounds that circumstances have arisen that "affect its supreme interests or the peace and security of one or more Contracting Parties." The Rarotonga Treaty requires a withdrawing state to show that there had been a violation by a Party "of a provision . . . essential to the achievement" of treaty objectives and to give notice twelve months in advance of withdrawal. As mentioned earlier, the United States has opposed the Rarotonga Treaty for fear that it would encourage the establishment of nuclear free zones in other parts of the world, a development that could greatly reduce the effectiveness of U.S. strategic capabilities.

The ASEAN proposal for a Southeast Asian Nuclear Weapon Free Zone, the SEA-NWFZ, is in part inspired by the Rarotonga Treaty, although it follows logically from ASEAN's concept of the Zone of Peace, Freedom and Neutrality (ZOPFAN) enunciated in 1971. The SEA-NWFZ was proposed in the ASEAN Ministerial Meeting of July 1984 in Jakarta as a concrete means of implementing the ZOPFAN concept, and it adopted from the SPNFZ a number of ideas on ways to handle the more complicated issues. The SEA-NWFZ was also seen as a regional approach and contribution to global disarmament efforts. The Third ASEAN Summit in Manila in December 1987 reiterated the members' commitment to SEA-NWFZ, to pursuit of global disarmament, and to the strengthening of the Nuclear Non-Proliferation Treaty. However, ASEAN leaders recognized that an untimely establishment of the SEA-NWFZ may in fact have a negative impact upon global disarmament efforts because of its asymmetrical effect upon the global strategic postures of the two superpowers.[7]

In view of the above, ASEAN has agreed to implement the SEA-NWFZ proposal gradually and by taking account of global security develop-

---

[7] See Jusuf Wanandi, "Security Development in Southeast Asia: An Indonesian View," paper presented at the Bicentennial Conference on "Australia and the World: Prologue and Prospects," Canberra, December 6-9, 1988.

ments—especially the central balance as affected by the outcome of negotiations on short-range battlefield weapons, strategic weapons, and conventional forces, as well as progress on confidence-building measures between the United States and the Soviet Union. ASEAN's decision to defer implementation of the SEA-NWFZ can be attributed in part to the need to maintain an international environment that can accommodate the denuclearization of the South Pacific. The reasons for ASEAN's decision are as follows: (a) The establishment of the SEA-NWFZ would increase opposition to the SPNFZ, particularly since similar NWFZs have also been mentioned for Northeast Asia, Central Europe, the Baltic Sea, and Mediterranean Sea regions. (b) The strategic implications of the SEA-NWFZ are far more serious than those of SPNFZ, given the strategic sea-lanes in Southeast Asian waters. (c) The SPNFZ is of much greater psychological and political importance to the countries in the South Pacific than SEA-NWFZ is to ASEAN nations. In the final analysis, the weighing of costs and benefits suggests that the maintenance of an international environment with SPNFZ and, for the time being, without SEA-NWFZ, would serve ASEAN's own interests as well.

Apart from the two regional issues examined above, there are other matters that could have strategic implications for the South Pacific. One is the presence of Libya in the region. It is difficult to make the case that legitimizes Libya's active presence in the region. Even if Libya's activities here turn out to be less extensive than those it undertook in the southern Philippines, southern Thailand, or in the Caribbean, they could have greater destabilizing effects upon these small island nations. Libya's intervention in the South Pacific, focused primarily on providing assistance to a small party in New Caledonia, the FULK (Front Uni de Liberation Kanak), appears to be in retaliation for France's intervention in Chad. Since 1984 Libya has given military and political training in Tripoli to a number of Kanak activists. However, leaders of the main pro-independence coalition, the FLNKS (Front de Liberation Nationale Kanak et Socialist), do not support these ties with Libya.

Vanuatu provides another opportunity for Libya to implement Khadafi's theories of national liberation and development which have lost their appeal in other parts of the world. Libya has sponsored two international conferences in Tripoli, attended by representatives of liberation movements from a number of Asian and Pacific countries. Perhaps the second meeting which was held in April 1987 will be the last one.[8] In response to a strong protest by Australia, Vanuatu has not given permission to Libya to open a diplomatic mission in Port Vila. Internal political disagreements among Vanuatu leaders have greatly reduced Libya's chances for activity in Vanuatu, and perhaps in the entire region. The more favorable developments in New Caledonia in 1988 have also reduced Libya's appeal. Libya

---

[8] Hegarty, op. cit.

has also attempted to develop relations with OPM, the Papuan Independence Movement, a dissident group that operates along the borders between Irian Jaya and Papua New Guinea. The extent of assistance given to this group is not known. OPM leaders have denied that they have any links with Libya. Overall, it is quite likely that Libya's influence in the South Pacific will continue to diminish, but the Libyan experience clearly shows that it does not require a high-cost operation to destabilize the small island nations in the South Pacific.

By the same token, this should also suggest that it does not take much of a financial burden to develop constructive relations with the South Pacific island countries. Such undertakings should be well within the reach of ASEAN countries. Since 1979, ASEAN has explored ways to promote relations with the South Pacific Forum. The task of developing relations and cooperation at the working level was given to the ASEAN Secretariat and the South Pacific Bureau for Economic Cooperation (SPEC). Areas of cooperation have been identified to include trade, industrial development, energy, and shipping. In its 1982 Ministerial Meeting, ASEAN agreed that various proposals be studied and plans for cooperation be drafted by the various ASEAN committees. However, to date the process has been highly disappointing. The reason is not a lack of political will, but perhaps lies simply in the lack of a workable institutional infrastructure: the status and authority of the ASEAN Secretariat are weaker than they are in the case of the SPEC of the South Pacific Forum.[9]

However, there are other channels of cooperation that can be developed between ASEAN and SPF. One important vehicle for cooperation is the so-called Human Resources Development (HRD), which operates under the auspices of the ASEAN-Pacific Forum and is sponsored by ASEAN and its Pacific dialogue partners (Australia, Canada, Japan, New Zealand, and the United States), with the cooperation also of the European Community. Indeed, most of the training programs designed under this project have been selected with a view to the needs of the South Pacific countries. Also, the Asia Pacific Development Center (APDC) in Kuala Lumpur has cooperated with SPEC in a joint study of opportunities in investment and joint-venture activities among the ASEAN countries and the South Pacific Island countries. Cooperation between ASEAN and the South Pacific countries has also been facilitated by the activities of the Pacific Economic Cooperation Conference (PECC), particularly in the area of fisheries development.

In addition, development cooperation has been undertaken on a bilateral basis. Technical cooperation between Indonesia and Papua New Guinea in the framework of TCDC (Technical Cooperation among Developing

---

[9] See C.P.F. Luhulima, "ASEAN-South Pacific Forum Dialogue: Prospects for Inter-Regional Cooperation," paper presented at the First Conference on "The Relationship between Indonesia and the South Pacific Countries," Hasanuddin University, December 5, 1988.

Countries) is one such successful example and has been given priority on the Indonesian side. Indeed, the strengthening of relations between Indonesia and Papua New Guinea in general over the past several years illustrates at its best the success of cooperation through promotion of mutual understanding and a sense of regional solidarity. Indonesia and Papua New Guinea share a common border, and their collaborative efforts could become a symbol for greater cooperation between ASEAN and the South Pacific region.

Relations between Indonesia and Papua New Guinea have greatly improved over the years and are excellent today. This is a remarkable development, because only a few years ago the relationship was on the brink of a severe crisis. Problems of border crossing have always existed and essentially are not of great concern insofar as they involve "traditional border crossers," namely movements across the borders of people who traditionally belong to a community, either a tribe or a group based on kinship. The territorial border itself is often not well defined and, given the terrain, not well marked. Thus, these problems are unavoidable. The main problem arises because of the operations along the border areas carried out by OPM, the Papuan Independence Movement, whose cadres often seek sanctuary inside Papua New Guinea where PNG troops have not been able to deal effectively with them.[10] In 1984 and 1985, the OPM launched a political campaign that resulted in a massive border crossing, involving some 12,000 people moving from Irian Jaya into Papua New Guinea. It was the magnitude of the problem at that juncture that compelled the government in Port Moresby to take drastic action, which eventually helped to bring about a successful resolution of the problem. First, the PNG government arrested a number of important OPM leaders and deported them. Second, it invited the UNHCR (United Nations High Commissioner on Refugees) to assist in resolving the problem. Third, it helped resettle some of the border crossers who remained behind.

The need to strengthen relations between the two countries has become a top priority on both sides in view of the problems resulting from the sharing of a difficult common border. Strong political will in Jakarta and Port Moresby led to the signing of a Treaty of Mutual Respect, Friendship and Cooperation between the two countries in 1986. Nevertheless, both sides have been too preoccupied with other matters to give sufficient attention to the development of mutual understanding and cooperation. Development efforts in Indonesia, for example, have been focused on the western part of the country, which contains most of the population and resources. Also, the external threat to the security of the country is perceived to come mainly from west of the country. In addition, the pattern of Indonesia's foreign relations has been pretty much influenced by its

---

[10]Stephen Mokis, "A Papua New Guinea Security Viewpoint and Its Implications on PNG-Australia Relations," paper presented at the Bicentennial Conference on "Australia and the World: Prologue and Prospects," Canberra, December 6-9, 1988.

economic relations that are mostly with the East Asian countries and the industrialized world, to the neglect of its neighbors in the South Pacific region.

It has only been since the beginning of the 1980s that Indonesia has accorded higher priorities to the development of its eastern areas, partly because the western part has now achieved a significant level of development. Allegations have been made that the eastern part, which is mainly inhabited by Melanesians, is discriminated against. Rather, the initial focus on the western part has simply been a matter of priority, given the country's scarce resources. In terms of direct financial transfers from the central government, the province of Irian Jaya has always ranked among the top recipients on a per capita basis. It should be noted that Irian Jaya became part of Indonesia only in 1963, and this fact was not internationally recognized until 1969. Therefore, in terms of nation-building in the framework of Indonesia's principle of "unity in diversity," Irian Jaya still lags behind the other regions. The insistence on a concept of nation based strictly on ethnicity was the origin of the OPM movement which initially received unqualified support from many South Pacific nations on the basis of ethnic solidarity.

Indonesia's ties with Australia have also improved considerably in recent years; they are as important as Indonesian-PNG ties to the maintenance of sound relations between Southeast Asia and the South Pacific. It is generally agreed that the maintenance of regional stability into the future requires the development of a strong triangular relationship among Indonesia, Papua New Guinea, and Australia.[11]

Conclusions

The entire South Pacific region is undergoing significant changes, largely as a result of some dynamic developments within these relatively young nations. The limited economic base of most of them has become a great source of frustration that in turn could have wide-ranging political implications. To most of these nations, small is not beautiful; if anything, it is a curse and is seen as the cause for their extreme dependence upon the outside world economically, which makes them also prone to outside political interventions. The ASEAN economies are in a far better position in terms of economic resources and other factors, such as population, history, and foreign relations. However, they also have gone through similar anxieties, and therefore can appreciate these grave concerns on the part of their South Pacific neighbors. This suggests the importance of nurturing political relations between the ASEAN countries and the South

---

[11] See J. Soedjati Djiwandono, "Indonesia's Relations with Australia and Papua New Guinea: An Overview," *The Indonesian Quarterly*, Vol. XIV, No. 2, July 1986.

Pacific countries; such relations may even be more valuable than economic relations.

The foreign policy agendas of these island countries logically emphasize the need for diversifying their relationships. The desire to reduce their dependence on Australia and New Zealand is often misunderstood. Australia and New Zealand, as an integral part of the South Pacific region, are their immediate neighbors and their most natural partners. Perhaps it is their overwhelming presence that causes some uneasiness. However, more equal relationships can emerge in the future, especially if these island nations succeed in diversifying their relations with other nations.

Although the younger, new generation of leaders has adopted a more nationalistic posture, these leaders are not necessarily anti-West as often perceived from the outside. Their stance toward New Caledonia's independence cannot be compromised; nor can their commitment to a regional nuclear free zone, which they see as a declaration that they want to continue to exist. Indeed, despite their smallness, these nations have every right to exist in safety and security. They also deserve sufficient understanding from their neighbors and from the United States. The South Pacific region's strategic importance rests not only on its location on the world's map, but perhaps more so on how well its inhabitants can interact with the world.

The Soviet Union, China, and the Pacific Islands

by John C. Dorrance

The North Pacific has often been characterized as an "American Lake" while the South Pacific has been described as an "ANZUS Lake." Although these characterizations remain generally apt from a strictly military point of view, political change within the region and new external influences assure that the regionally-involved Western powers can no longer rely on comfortable past assumptions of Pacific island state biases toward their interests. The buildup of Soviet Pacific forces also has "polluted" the American Lake. Among the many new external players—some positive and some negative—complicating the regional political fabric are Libya, Indonesia, Singapore, Malaysia, Israel, South Korea, North Korea, the Federal Republic of Germany, Japan, Taiwan, Vietnam, Cuba, Canada, the Soviet Union, the People's Republic of China, the European Community, and other political and economic organizations—some private and some governmental. This paper attempts to assess the regional interests, objectives, policies, and activities of the Soviet Union and the People's Republic of China, likely future directions, and Western responses—both current and potential.[1]

The Strategic Environment

One persistent theme has characterized external power interest and competition in the Pacific islands since the first European sighting by Magellan in 1521. The islands, with few exceptions, were perceived as having little intrinsic exploitable value other than their relationship to

---

[1] Most of the data and analysis provided in this assessment are based on the author's exposure to the subject as a U.S. Foreign Service Officer dealing with the region. Where appropriate and possible, public sources are also cited. Additionally, I have drawn on the expertise of several Australian regional scholars. In particular, see: Richard Herr, "Soviet and Chinese Interests in the Pacific Islands," a paper presented on May 19, 1989, at a conference on Strategic Cooperation and Competition in the Pacific Islands, National Defense University, Washington, D.C.; David Hegarty, "The Soviet Union in the South Pacific in the 1990s," in Ross Babbage, editor, *The Soviets in the Pacific in the 1990s* (Sydney, Australia: Pergamon Press, 1989); Paul Dibb, "Soviet Strategy Towards Australia, New Zealand and the Southwest Pacific," *Australian Outlook*, Vol. 39, No. 2, August 1985, pp. 69-76; and Owen Harries, *Strategy and the Southwest Pacific: An Australian Perspective* (Sydney, Australia: Pacific Security Research Institute, 1989).

trans-Pacific lanes of communication. But that value alone has made the Pacific islands an arena for varying degrees of strategic competition for over 400 years. In World War II, allied and Japanese forces fought across the island stepping-stones of trans-Pacific routes. At the close of the Pacific War, the Micronesian islands of the North Pacific previously controlled by Japan—the Northern Marianas, the Marshalls, and the Carolines—came under U.S. administration as a "strategic" UN trusteeship: the Trust Territory of the Pacific Islands (TTPI). Washington was determined that no military adversary would ever again have access to these islands for attacks on the United States and its allies, or for interdiction of trans-Pacific routes. The ANZUS powers have pursued similar exclusionary objectives in the South Pacific.

Changing military, transport, and communications technologies have lessened the importance of the islands as "stepping-stones," but other strategic interests have emerged. For the United States, the Kwajalein Missile Range facility in the Marshall islands is essential for the testing of ICBMs and development of the Strategic Defense Initiative. Guam, Palau, and the Northern Mariana islands have potential significance as "fall-back" sites for some activities presently located in the Philippines. Guam already is a critical element of U.S. Western Pacific force deployments. To the South, Indonesia and the Melanesian island states, particularly Papua New Guinea, still dominate the strategic approaches to Australia. The World War II Japanese thrust southward through these islands toward Australia permanently established that point in Australian strategic analysis. Australian defense forces and strategy today are structured on the premise that any direct threat to Australia will be from or through these islands. France asserts that continuing access to its nuclear test site in French Polynesia is essential for its independent nuclear forces. (American and British nuclear testing in the Pacific islands ended in 1962.)

The region's continuing strategic relevance, and the potential for new threats were primary considerations in the 1951 establishment of the ANZUS alliance with its focus on Pacific security, including treaty provisions triggering security commitments in the event of an attack or the threat of an attack on the forces or territories of any of the parties anywhere in the Pacific.

A relatively recent Western concern, with the Soviet Union's development of a major Pacific naval capability, has been a war scenario involving the mining of the Strait of Malacca and the Indonesian straits linking the Pacific and Indian Oceans. The South Pacific and the straits north and south of Australia would then become the primary alternate linkage of the two oceans, with the potential for Soviet submarine interdiction of shipping, and a corollary potential Western requirement for access to island airfields for anti-submarine warfare. A possible future security interest (discussed in detail in another chapter) is the potential importance of the South Pacific relative to any future U.S. development of an anti-satellite warfare capability.

The ongoing decolonization of the Pacific islands, begun in 1962 and now nearly complete, added a new dimension to ANZUS regional strategic and political interests and objectives—that of encouraging the emergence of democratic states which, though not formally aligned with the West, would be receptive to Western security requirements, including ANZUS naval and air access, and exclusion of any adversary military access and political influence. The latter objective came to be described as "strategic denial." It translated into exclusion of any form of Soviet presence within the Pacific islands. It was generally successful until the Gorbachev era, but was never applied to the People's Republic of China.

Although improving East-West relations and the receding threat of East-West conflict are realities, so is the fact that the Soviet Union will remain the West's most dangerous potential adversary. In these circumstances, most of the foregoing factors will remain relevant in the context of continuing Western deterrence of conflict strategies.

The Soviet Union: Regional Interests and Objectives

From a Western perspective, the Soviet Union has been the only significant strategic competitor in the Pacific islands since World War II. Much of that competition has been more potential than actual. Prior to 1962 all of the islands were colonies, dependent territories, protectorates, or UN trust territories of Western powers; only with decolonization has there been the possibility of Soviet access. Even with decolonization, the political arrangements in the North Pacific in 1986 between the United States and the freely-associated states of Micronesia (the Republic of the Marshall Islands, the Federated States of Micronesia, and potentially Palau), and U.S. territorial and commonwealth relationships with Guam and the Northern Mariana islands, assure no Soviet military access, and limited potential for political access. The political inclinations of South Pacific island states similarly inhibit Soviet military access and significant political influence.

Within the broader Asia/Pacific region, the Pacific islands undoubtedly are a distant fourth Soviet strategic/political priority after China, Japan, and Korea; Southeast Asia; and Australia and New Zealand. Major Soviet national security interests do not exist in the South Pacific—except with respect to the ANZUS alliance and Australian-American joint defense facilities in Australia. (The latter are essential not only for verification of arms control agreements and early warning of Soviet missile launches, but also for U.S. and Australian communication with submarines operating in the Pacific and Indian Oceans, and for intelligence related to war-fighting capabilities.)

Unlike the Western powers active in the Pacific islands, the Soviet Union has pursued its regional objectives from a zero-base: no territorial presence, no resident diplomatic representation, no military presence, no ideological affinity, no investment links, and insignificant trade levels. Prior to the peaking of the decolonization cycle in the mid-1970s, Moscow's regionally-related activities had been limited to attacks in the United Nations and elsewhere on regional decolonization processes and objectives (particularly those relating to the U.S. administered TTPI); intensive hydrographic and oceanographic research related to marine resources and submarine warfare requirements; intelligence collection directed at the Kwajalein Missile Range facility and French nuclear testing; and encouragement of regional antinuclear emotions directed at French nuclear testing and U.S. Navy port access.

Paralleling the above activities, Moscow in the 1960s began a substantial build-up of Pacific naval and air assets—a process that accelerated in the 1970s and 1980s. However, a coherent set of regional policy objectives and a related strategy for the Pacific islands began to emerge only in the mid-1970s. By 1986 and Gorbachev's Vladivostok speech on Soviet interests and policies in the Asia/Pacific region, Western governments had discerned a clear pattern of Soviet objectives in or related to the Pacific islands:

- Elimination or at least reduction of Western naval superiority in the Pacific through arms control initiatives.

- Related to the foregoing, restraints on Western (but especially U.S.) military capabilities through political denial of port and air access in the region.

- De-coupling of Australia and New Zealand from the Western alliance system (a long-standing objective in some measure now achieved in New Zealand, although not a direct consequence of Soviet action).

- Western and regional state acceptance of the Soviet Union as a Pacific power with legitimate regional interests.

- Erosion of Western influence and promotion of island state nonalignment.

- Establishment of a resident diplomatic presence in the Pacific islands.

- Access to regional marine resources (particularly tuna), and to commercial shipping and trade opportunities.

With the exception of access to regional fisheries, the potential for seabed minerals mining, and shipping and trade opportunities, all Soviet objectives in the Pacific islands relate to the global East-West competition, to Soviet interests in the broader Asia/Pacific region, and to Moscow's determination to advance the reality of the Soviet Union as a global power through a presence and influence in all global regions.

The Emerging Soviet Presence

"On-the-ground" Soviet pursuit of regional objectives began in 1976 with proposals for the establishment of a Soviet embassy in Tonga, a fisheries fleet base in the same state, Aeroflot access for crew exchanges and resupply, and Soviet construction of a dock and expansion of Tonga's major airport. (The Soviet Union had already established diplomatic relations with many key island states, including Tonga, but with non-resident diplomatic representation based in Wellington or Canberra.) Tongan conservatism and suspicion, and Australian and New Zealand pressure, assured a turn-down of the proposal—but necessitated off-set increases in Australian and New Zealand development assistance to Tonga. (Ironically, New Zealand in 1978 did provide to the Soviet Union that which it had counseled Tonga against: a fisheries agreement with shore access and limited related facilities. The application of a double standard did not go unnoticed in the Pacific islands.)

The Tonga episode triggered a major reassessment by Canberra and Wellington of the Soviet regional political threat. Two consequences were expansion of Australia's and New Zealand's regional diplomatic presence and development assistance programs (Australia's aid programs were quadrupled), and pressure on Washington to play a more active secondary role in the South Pacific. That pressure in turn generated Washington decisions in 1977 and 1978 to establish a small regional development assistance program, new educational and cultural exchange programs, and a first coherent Pacific islands policy. If nothing else, the "Russians are coming" syndrome had focused new ANZUS interest on the South Pacific.

In a series of ANZUS consultations, it was agreed that Soviet efforts to establish a regional presence would be countered by increases in development assistance and trade promotion efforts, and support for strengthened regional institutions (in part to minimize prospects for aberrant micro-state behavior). Australia and New Zealand would continue to play the lead alliance role in the South Pacific, but with the United States strengthening its supportive role.[2] The United States would continue to play the lead Western role in the islands north of the equator, its traditional area of presence and influence.

Subsequent pre-Gorbachev Soviet efforts to establish a diplomatic presence in other states and to conclude other fisheries or trade arrangements were all rebuffed, at least in part because of regional reactions to

---

[2] Herr, op. cit., p. 8.

the Soviet invasion of Afghanistan in 1979, but also because of crude, ideologically-oriented diplomacy that offered little appeal to conservative island governments. Early Soviet efforts at regional penetration also were hampered by ignorance of the region, including a tendency to interpret all regional political developments and issues in the context of dogmatic "class struggle" and East-West ideological conflict. A marginal measure of regional access was achieved in the late 1970s when Soviet cruise ships began operating under charter to Australian tour organizations. However, even these arrangements were terminated for several years as a regional response to the Soviet invasion of Afghanistan. More recently, with the major expansion of the Soviet merchant marine, the latter has become a factor in Pacific trade, including that involving the Pacific islands.

A classic implementation of the ANZUS decision to deny any form of Soviet access to the region occurred in 1980. In that year the Soviet Academy of Sciences offered to the regional Committee for the Coordination of Joint Prospecting for Mineral Resources in the South Pacific (CCOP/SOPAC) a five-year marine resource research project involving two annual research cruises and port access throughout the Pacific islands. The offer was initially accepted, but then rejected following discussions among the ANZUS partners and a counter-offer of a similar American-Australian-New Zealand project. Washington, Canberra, and Wellington were concerned with three dimensions of the project: the potential military applications of the research, the potential for political meddling flowing from port access, and the precedent of any form of Soviet regional access.

Parallel to the foregoing Soviet initiatives, Soviet South Pacific hydro-graphic/oceanographic research, begun in 1957, intensified; by the 1980s Moscow had accumulated the world's most comprehensive data base on the Pacific Ocean. Surveillance of the Kwajalein Missile Range facility and French nuclear testing also increased throughout this period, and continues at a high level. In the early 1960s, Soviet research vessels, operating under the guise of International Geophysical Year projects, also conducted extensive geomagnetic surveys essential to accurate ICBM targeting of major regional airports and ports. Ironically, potential target ports hosted visits by these vessels.

Yet another and continuing dimension of Soviet regional activity was intensification of "disinformation" relating to U.S. military planning for and related activities in Micronesia. The Marshall Islands, the Federated States of Micronesia, and Palau were all moving toward free association with the United States, with provision for continuing U.S. defense responsibility. A classic case, particularly in the 1980s, has been a steady drumbeat of Moscow assertions that the United States seeks to coerce Palau into free association so that it might base Trident submarines and ICBMs in those islands. The facts that the free association agreement with Palau prohibits these actions, and that Trident submarines and ICBMs are never based outside the United States, have been ignored. Nonetheless, the allegations have obtained widespread credence in the region, and Palau's relationship with the United States has become a major cause of regional peace groups.

In the political arena, penetration efforts increased with invitations to island students, trade union leaders, and antinuclear activists to visit the Soviet Union for conferences, education, or short-term training.

The Gorbachev Era and Regional Turning Points

The beginning of the Gorbachev era in 1985 coincided with regional developments providing new opportunities and a more positive atmosphere for Soviet initiatives. Foremost, perhaps, has been generational change in island state political leadership. The first generation of post-colonial leaders was being replaced by new elites generally better educated, less conservative, more nationalistic and assertive, and often more resentful of aid-dependency on and related political influence by a narrow range of traditional Western donors—especially Australia and New Zealand, but also the United States. (In all but three of the region's 21 states and dependent territories, external assistance is equivalent to 25 to 100 percent or more of gross domestic product.) Still conservative by most Third World standards, these emerging elites are nonetheless more prone to experiment with new international linkages—if only to demonstrate independent foreign policies, diversify economic dependency and related influences, and expand export trade opportunities. As always, the small numbers of elites involved in island government foreign policy decision-making, and in leadership of public opinion on related issues, operates to the advantage of those seeking to manipulate island state policies. The smallness and fragility of some island states also contributes to vulnerability.

In more recent years, global changes in East-West relations and associated perceptions of a receding threat of conflict, reform and turmoil within the Soviet Union, the Soviet withdrawal from Afghanistan, and Moscow's tolerance of the democratization processes in Eastern Europe have been responsible for some erosion of the traditional suspicion of Moscow's regional objectives and activities.

With the election of Labor governments in Australia and New Zealand in 1983 and 1984, new life was given to widespread regional sentiment for a nuclear-free zone and termination of French nuclear testing. The 1986 Treaty of Rarotonga establishing the South Pacific Nuclear Free Zone (SPNFZ) was one major consequence. Although the relatively conservative Australian Labor Government assured that SPNFZ is compatible with essential U.S. regional security interests and requirements (e.g., no impediments to regional access by nuclear-armed or -powered ships), the

United States, Britain, and France refused to adhere to the related protocols, while the Soviet Union and the People's Republic of China promptly did adhere. That contrast significantly improved Moscow's regional image, particularly since regional states assumed that the SPNFZ treaty satisfied basic U.S. criteria for participation, and thus anticipated U.S. adherence.

Separately from the foregoing, the New Zealand Labor Government in early 1985 implemented "nuclear-free" policies that had the effect of banning the U.S. Navy from New Zealand's ports and waters. The United States responded with suspension of its ANZUS obligations to and defense cooperation with New Zealand. These developments were applauded by Moscow and cited as appropriate precedents for Australia and the island states. An unfortunate side effect was erosion of traditional trilateral ANZUS policy coordination and consultations on regional developments. New Zealand's actions also tended to lend legitimacy to existing proclivities in some island states to adopt similar nuclear-free policies.

During the same time-frame, Kanak pressures in New Caledonia for independence began to peak with inter-communal ethnic violence verging on insurrection and repressive responses from the then conservative government in Paris. Regional outrage intensified with the 1985 French bombing and sinking of the Greenpeace *Rainbow Warrior* in Auckland harbor—an act of state terrorism by anyone's definition. The tardiness and softness of Washington's reaction to that incident, a perception that the United States had not adhered to the SPNFZ treaty protocols because of support for French nuclear testing in French Polynesia, and a perception of American tolerance for French repressive measures in New Caledonia played into Moscow's hands. These perceptions were reinforced by Radio Moscow broadcasts to the region, and by visiting Soviet diplomats.

An especially damaging development for the U.S. image in the late 1970s through the mid-1980s—from which the Soviets gained benefit—was the tuna fisheries jurisdiction dispute described in other papers in this volume. Essentially, the United States did not recognize island state jurisdiction over tuna within their 200-mile oceanic Exclusive Economic Zones (EEZs). American tuna clippers thus "pirated" (from a regional perspective) the single major commercial resource of some island states. The issue culminated in 1984 with the Solomon Islands' seizure of the American tuna clipper *Jeanette Diana*, and retaliatory U.S. economic sanctions. Regional outrage against the United States quickly reached high levels, and receded only in 1987 with conclusion of a regional fisheries agreement between the United States and the member states of the South Pacific Forum Fisheries Agency. The imbroglio provided a new opening for Soviet fisheries initiatives.

In 1985 Kiribati concluded a fisheries agreement with the Soviet Union providing for access to the former's EEZ for an annual fee of US$1.5 million, but not for shore access by either Soviet trawlers or Aeroflot. The Soviet payments represented about 15 percent of Kiribati's budget, an obviously significant inducement. As Kiribati's President commented, why not take Soviet money for what the Russians, like the Americans, can take, if they choose, without compensation.[3] The ANZUS capitals, but particularly Canberra, had been concerned not only by the general precedent of formalized regional access with its political implications, but also that shore access, if subsequently provided, would offer opportunities for political meddling. Canberra and Wellington thus actively opposed the Kiribati agreement, while Washington counseled caution in dealing with the Soviets. A senior U.S. defense official also publicly expressed concern for the potential establishment of ground-based intelligence facilities directed at Kwajalein, and other facilities that could advantage Soviet military satellite programs, Pacific missile testing, or new Soviet air routes to Central America.[4] These concerns were considered less than credible by most island governments.

A year later a similar agreement was concluded with Vanuatu, but with provision for periodic trawler shore access for resupply and crew rest. Both agreements were aborted after their first year when the Soviets argued that the tuna catch was not economic and insisted upon fee reductions. One knowledgeable Australian source estimates that the Kiribati agreement netted a catch valued at only US$1.7 million while the overall annual cost of fleet operations had been about US$15 million. The Soviet Union's Vanuatu venture apparently was even worse, at least in terms of economic return.[5]

For the longer term, both agreements may have been politically productive for the Soviets in that their performance did tend to ease concern that they would fish for more than fish. Most observers now agree that the Soviets adhered meticulously to the agreements and did not engage in any untoward activities. However, Soviet officials, including Foreign Minister Shevardnadze, have confirmed that an intended objective of trade and fisheries agreements, aside from tuna protein, has been Soviet political access and influence.[6] In that context more recent Soviet efforts to conclude fisheries agreements with other island states, principally Papua New Guinea but also the Solomons and Fiji, remain a Western concern. Papua New Guinea did initial a draft agreement in principle with the Soviet Union in late 1989, including provision for shore access.

---

[3] Keynote address by Kiribati President Tabai at the September 7, 1986, opening of the Waigani Seminar, University of Papua New Guinea, Port Moresby, Papua New Guinea..

[4] U.S. Information Agency Wireless File, September 10, 1986.

[5] Hegarty, op cit., pp. 115-116, 124-125.

[6] Ibid., p. 118.

Coincident with its first fisheries successes, the Soviet Union signaled new political, economic, and security interests in the Asia/Pacific region, including the Pacific islands, by way of Gorbachev's 1986 Vladivostok speech and subsequent statements in Krasnoyarsk and elsewhere. In one form or another, explicitly or implicitly, previously cited Soviet regional interests and objectives were reaffirmed. There has been, however, a reduced emphasis on ideological competition, and new emphasis on political and economic pragmatism. As with Soviet foreign policy generally, diplomacy in the Pacific islands now is more knowledgeable and conciliatory, and less confrontational—and thus far more effective. Soviet officials visiting island states currently stress that there are no "evil intentions" behind the development of "normal relations"—a point also emphasized by the Soviet Union to Australia and New Zealand because of their regional strategic concerns.

New sophistication in Soviet regional diplomacy also reflects "new thinking" in Third World policies—a shift away from doctrinaire ideological approaches and support for Marxist-Leninist regimes toward more active pursuit of relationships with and influence in a broader range of developing countries. According to this "new thinking," particular attention is to be given to states, even though they may be on a capitalist course, which have grievances with the United States and other Western powers. One Soviet official has commented that the West's tendency to act "crudely" or "brazenly" in Third World countries produces reactions that make cooperation with Moscow especially attractive.[7] Without question, the Soviet Union has recognized that, in the case of the Pacific islands, a small investment in sensitivity and resources can yield significant dividends.

The application of these principles is illustrated in part by a regional diplomacy that continues to focus on nuclear concerns (e.g., French nuclear testing and the British, French, and U.S. failure to adhere to the SPNFZ treaty protocols), French Pacific colonial policies, the Palau issue, island state frustration with aid dependency, a related search for diversification of economic links and new export trade opportunities, and regional concerns relating to enmeshment in superpower rivalry and potential conflict.

Implementation of "new thinking" and pursuit of related traditional objectives over the past five years has included a surge in visits by Soviet officials and delegations seeking not only new fisheries agreements, but also establishment of diplomatic missions, cultural exchanges, economic joint ventures, and new trade relationships. Invitations to regional political leaders to visit the Soviet Union are more frequent, and some have been accepted—as have been more offers of scholarships, short-term training,

---

[7] Ibid., p. 120. Also, Thomas J. Zamostny, "Moscow and the Third World: Recent Trends in Soviet Thinking," *Soviet Studies*, Vol. XXXVI, No. 2, April 1984, p. 233.

and conference participation. The major success in this new drive for closer regional relationships and a related diplomatic presence has been the establishment of a Soviet Embassy in Papua New Guinea in 1990.

The Military Dimension

Although the easing of East-West tensions is a reality, so is the formidable buildup of Soviet Pacific naval and air power over the past twenty years—to the point that the Soviet Pacific fleet is now the largest of the Soviet Navy's four fleets with some 144 surface combatants, 118 submarines, and several hundred auxiliary vessels. The Soviets also base several thousand naval and air force aircraft in the Far East, including several hundred long-range strategic bombers equipped with cruise missiles. Political reform in the Soviet Union and actual or planned reductions in ground and missile forces have not yet been matched by changes in these capabilities. The Department of Defense does anticipate that Soviet naval forces will be reduced by retiring a number of aging submarines and destroyers and replacing them with fewer but far more capable ships—but that overall capabilities will be enhanced rather than reduced.[8]

Soviet naval operations in the Pacific thus far have been largely confined to the North and Western Pacific, and excursions into the Indian Ocean, with resupply and refitting capabilities at Cam Ranh Bay in Vietnam. The past several years also have seen a significant decline in Soviet Pacific naval operations, that is, fewer "steaming days" and less activity at Cam Ranh Bay. These changes have been driven by economic restraints rather than strategic considerations.

Western, particularly U.S., Pacific air and naval assets for the most part remain quantitatively and qualitatively superior to those of the Soviet Union. The latter would be hard pressed to sustain offensive naval operations distant from Soviet Far Eastern waters, with one major exception applicable to the South Pacific. The Soviet Union does have a significant capability to conduct anti-shipping mine warfare, including in the Strait of Malacca and the Indonesian straits linking the Pacific and Indian oceans, and to conduct antishipping warfare throughout the Pacific with its some 83 attack submarines. The Soviet Air Force and naval aviation also could interdict shipping and allied naval forces throughout much of the Pacific from bases in the Soviet Far East, and possibly Cam Ranh Bay. With these exceptions, most Western defense analysts agree that Soviet Pacific naval capabilities are best suited for protection of the Sea of Okhotsk bastion of 26 strategic missile submarines—the latter very much an offensive nuclear strike system. As to Cam Ranh, prospects for its survival in any major conflict

---

[8] Data on the Soviet military buildup and capabilities are drawn primarily from *Soviet Military Power: Prospects for Change, 1989*, Department of Defense, Washington, D.C., 1989.

are bleak. There also are indications most Cam Ranh operations may be phased out in connection with economic constraints and broader regional political objectives.

At another level, Soviet ICBMs can be targeted on Australia, New Zealand, and the Pacific islands. Soviet officials (including former Deputy Foreign Minister Kapitsa) and other commentators have remarked that Soviet missiles are "reserved" for the critical U.S.-Australian joint defense facilities in Australia, and for regional ports hosting U.S. ships.[9] Although not related to the foregoing, the Soviet Union also uses the Pacific islands region as an impact area for ICBM tests—initially in the Central Pacific, and after 1975 in the North Pacific in an area close to Midway and Hawaii.

Given the disparity between Soviet and Western naval assets in the Pacific, and economic and technological restraints which assure a continuing imbalance in those forces, a primary Soviet strategic objective has been Pacific naval arms limitations agreements that would reduce or eliminate Western naval superiority. Soviet initiatives in this area have had little appeal in the West, particularly in Washington. While the Soviet Union is essentially a land-based power with few overseas defense commitments, the United States is a maritime power linked to Asian and Pacific allies and trading partners by trans-Pacific sea and air lanes. Five of the seven U.S. security alliances are with Asia/Pacific states, and nearly half of all U.S. foreign trade transits the Pacific. However, U.S. budgetary restraints inevitably will result in some reduction in U.S. Pacific deployments and capabilities. There may be some scope for arms limitations arrangements in that context—although not to the point of parity in Soviet and U.S. naval forces.

Linked to the foregoing, an Australian observer notes that Soviet spokesmen have pressed the concept of "equal security" in the South Pacific in an attempt to encourage island states to see their security interests as being best served by excluding both superpowers—in reality, excluding the United States, in the absence of any present or likely future Soviet military access.[10] Such a theme was pressed by Gorbachev in his 1986 Vladivostok speech, and in his 1987 *Merdeka* interview. He described "mutual renunciation" of naval exercises and maneuvers as a model that could be extended to the South Pacific.[11] In short, the Soviets press for the reverse of the ANZUS strategic denial objective: strategic denial of the region to the West in general and the United States in particular.

Similarly, in the North Pacific, the Soviet Union has opposed in the United Nations and elsewhere the conclusion of free association relationships

---

[9] For specific public statements and their sources, see Dibb, op. cit., p. 70.

[10] Hegarty, op. cit., p. 117.

[11] "Gorbachev *Merdeka* Interview: 'Global Double Zero' for Medium-Range Missiles," *Summary of World Broadcasts*, SU/8628/A3/1-9, July 24, 1987, p. 5.

between the United States and the Federated States of Micronesia, the Marshall Islands, and Palau—principally because that arrangement provides for U.S. defense responsibility for, and basing options or arrangements in, these islands. That stance has complicated international recognition of the status of these states. The Soviet Union has argued that full independence was the only appropriate outcome of the termination of the U.S. administered Trust Territory of the Pacific Islands. Faced with a certain Soviet veto of a UN Security Council resolution endorsing termination of the trusteeship agreement between the Council and the United States, Washington was forced in 1986 unilaterally to declare trusteeship termination for all elements of the trusteeship but Palau. Once internal Palauan constitutional restraints on implementation of a similar free association relationship are resolved, Washington undoubtedly will take the same unilateral action.

Meanwhile, though possessing a peace-time capability to project naval power into the South Pacific, the Soviets with rare exception (and then primarily with submarines) have refrained from such action—as well as from seeking naval port access or any land-based military facilities. In 1988 the Soviet First Deputy Chief of Naval Operations, Vice Admiral Dmitry Komarov, asserted that the Soviet Navy "rarely if ever exercises [its] right to freedom of navigation in the South Pacific." Also: "In the South Pacific one can only meet research vessels of the Soviet Navy . . . and also training ships that make voyages with cadets on board. We simply do not need to send our warships there."[12] Soviet Foreign Minister Shevardnadze, during a 1988 visit to Fiji, also asserted no Soviet interest in South Pacific military access.

Aside from the fact that no island state is likely to grant such access, Moscow has calculated that the absence of Soviet naval activity in the South Pacific lowers regional threat perceptions and thus encourages sentiment to the effect that ANZUS and a regional U.S. military presence are not relevant to regional security—or indeed may be a liability in the event of East-West conflict. A parallel calculation is that deployment into the South Pacific of Soviet naval forces and pressures for port or other access would be counterproductive vis-a-vis higher priority strategic objectives: Pacific naval arms control agreements, denial of regional U.S. Navy port access, closure of the joint defense facilities in Australia, decoupling of Australia, the Philippines, and Japan from their American alliances, and island state nonalignment.

To sum up, the Soviet Union, except for submarine warfare, has little in the way of either present or potential capabilities to mount offensive military operations in the South Pacific, and (at least for the foreseeable future) has no prospects for regional port or other military access. The primary Soviet

---

[12] Interview with Vice Admiral Dmitry Komarov, reported in *The Australian* newspaper, March 21, 1988, p. 13.

threat in the region is thus political—their efforts to accomplish denial to the United States of that which is not available to Moscow.

Soviet Surrogate Activities

Soviet regional objectives also have been marginally served by client or surrogate states: principally Vietnam, Cuba, North Korea, and Libya—although none has a resident diplomatic presence. The former three have had some measure of success in establishing diplomatic relations with key island states and, especially in the case of Vanuatu, sporadic official dialogue. Cuba in particular has been diplomatically active in that island state and is credited with Vanuatu's membership in the Non-Aligned Movement, the only island state thus far to have joined that grouping. Vietnam has provided modest assistance to Vanuatu in the form of medical teams. North Korean efforts to establish diplomatic dialogue with several island states for the most part have been rebuffed. All three linkages appear to have eroded in the past several years in the face of factional political strife in Vanuatu and the dismissal from government of Barak Sope, their most enthusiastic advocate.

The Libyan connection was of greater concern in the mid-1980s. Tripoli provided security and other training and finance to cadres from Vanuatu's principal political party, and to a radical fringe of the Kanak Liberation Movement in New Caledonia. However, the latter Libyan connection and those involved have been disavowed by the moderate mainstream Kanak leadership. Vanuatu's links with Libya also appear to have been reduced, and plans for the opening of a Libyan People's Bureau in that island state have been cancelled. There may be some continuing links between Libya and radical fringe elements in French Polynesia. The Australian and other regional governments believe that Libyan regional activity and influence currently are at the lowest levels since the mid-1980s. There is a general assumption that the primary Libyan regional objective has been trouble-making for the West in general, but particularly for France in retaliation for the French-Libyan confrontation in Chad. Taken together, most of the foregoing activities have been little more than a nuisance mandating careful monitoring.

By way of contrast, the regional activities of Soviet front organizations, surrogate Marxist and other leftist Australian and New Zealand trade union leaders, regional antinuclear peace groups, regional church organizations with objectives congruent with those of the Soviets, some leftist Australian and New Zealand television journalists and academics, and others with linkages into and influence within the Pacific islands have had a major regional impact. Their primary regional causes have been termination of the ANZUS alliance and of the joint defense facilities in Australia, promotion of a nuclear-free Pacific (including termination of U.S. regional naval and other military access and of French nuclear testing), promotion of France's political departure from the South Pacific through independence for New Caledonia and French Polynesia, and opposition to U.S. defense relationships with Palau and the Micronesian states in free association with the United States. Regional political and environmental concerns, for example, New Caledonia's independence and French nuclear testing, provide fertile ground for the activities of these groups.[13]

Foremost among regionally active Soviet front organizations is the World Federation of Trade Unions (WFTU), which operates primarily through Marxist and other leftist Australian trade unions and their leaders, and the Marxist-led New Zealand Council of Trade Unions (NZCTU)—formerly the New Zealand Federation of Labor. The NZCTU's president, Ken Douglas, also is active in the Moscow-oriented New Zealand Socialist Unity Party. A number of leftist Australian and New Zealand unions are affiliated with the WFTU's industry secretariats, and regularly participate in WFTU conferences. A few island trade unions have affiliated with the WFTU; those in New Caledonia, the Solomons, and Vanuatu are among the largest and most influential in the region.[14]

The WFTU at its 1978 Prague Conference determined to place a greater focus on the South Pacific. Establishment of the Pacific Trade Union Forum—now the Pacific Trade Union Community (PTUC)—followed in 1980 and has been dominated from the outset by Australian and New Zealand Marxists pressing a political agenda having everything to do with Soviet regional strategic and political objectives and little relationship to traditional labor concerns. A prominent Australian trade unionist, Michael Easson, points out that the PTUC is "the only major forum for regional union conferences and regional meetings of Pacific union leaders," and that it sets the agenda for many regional issues.[15] Fijian PTUC activists also were a significant component in the Fiji coalition government elected to office in 1987—but shortly afterward deposed by a military coup. The coalition government had contemplated adopting "nuclear-free" policies similar to those of New Zealand.

Other Soviet front organizations active in the region have included the World Peace Council, the Congress for International Cooperation and Disarmament, and the World Federation of Democratic Youth. Although not a Soviet front, the left-leaning World Council of Churches and its

---

[13] For an excellent overview of Soviet surrogate activity, see George Tanham, "Subverting the South Pacific," *The National Interest*, No. 11, Spring 1988, pp. 85-94. For details on related trade union activity, see Michael Easson, "Labor and the Left in the Pacific," in Dennis Bark and Owen Harries, editors, *The Red Orchestra* (Stanford, CA: Hoover Institution Press, 1989). I have drawn heavily on these sources.

[14] A small Fiji union affiliated with the WFTU in the early 1980s. That affiliation has since been terminated. Most island unions are affiliated with the ICFTU.

[15] Easson, op. cit.

regional affiliate, the Pacific Conference of Churches (PCC), have been advocates of liberation theology and related anti-Western objectives in the guise of decolonization and antinuclear activities. Although the PCC did play a valued role in the decolonization of Vanuatu, there has been a proclivity to manipulate legitimate regional concerns in ways that focus exclusively on Western rather than Soviet behavior, and that have the practical effect of Soviet surrogacy. As one example, calls are made for the closure of U.S. Pacific bases and termination of U.S. regional naval access while no mention is made of the Soviet presence in Cam Ranh Bay or the buildup of Soviet Pacific forces. There has been some decline in the influence of the PCC in recent years, in part because of dissatisfaction with its political agenda on the part of many regional churches, and a consequent reduction in its funding.

Antinuclear peace groups in Australia and New Zealand, often with links to and support from leftist trade unions, also independently pursue objectives paralleling Moscow's, with no tolerance of Western deterrence of conflict strategies. Closely associated with similar groups in the Pacific islands, their primary causes parallel those of the PTUC—including advocacy of unilateral disarmament.

Of considerable influence within Australia and New Zealand, but also to some degree within the Pacific islands, are a number of Australian and New Zealand leftist or otherwise anti-U.S. television journalists who provide a steady flow of "documentaries" (often little more than a refined regurgitation of Soviet disinformation) and other reporting sympathetic to Pacific peace group causes. Of greater significance in island states has been the presence of a number of leftist or otherwise anti-Western Australian, New Zealand, and other faculty members in regional tertiary educational institutions (but principally the University of the South Pacific in Fiji) from whence many of the Pacific islands' political elites have been emerging in the 1970s and 1980s.

All of these groups are prone to conspiracy theories of history and politics; they allege—and promote—the concepts (false) of CIA involvement in the 1987 overthrow of Fiji's elected government, and U.S. coercion of Palau into a free association relationship with the United States. Their primary sources of data and themes appear to be Soviet disinformation disseminated by various Soviet fronts.

The foregoing groups coalesced into the "Independent and Nuclear-Free Pacific Movement" in the 1970s. The movement's influence has been felt by regional state governments already concerned for the environmental impact of French nuclear testing and led to the first significant regional pressures for a South Pacific Nuclear Free Zone in the early and mid-1970s. That initiative died in 1975-1976 with the defeat of Labor governments in Australia and New Zealand, but re-emerged in 1983 and 1984 with the re-election of Labor governments. As previously indicated, Australia's new Labor Government, committed to the ANZUS alliance, made every effort to ensure that the 1986 SPNFZ Treaty did not conflict with essential U.S. security interests. Prime Minister Hawke considered the initiative an essential firebreak to contain regional and domestic pressures for a more radical SPNFZ treaty that would have done major damage to Western strategic interests.

In assessing the activities of Australian and New Zealand Marxists and other leftists and pacifists, it is important not to exaggerate their influence. Numerically they are small, and they are unlikely ever to govern either country. Nonetheless, they remain a potent force with influence out of proportion to their numbers—because of their control of many key trade unions, their strength in the policymaking conferences of Labor parties, and their disproportionate role in the media and academia. These influences were a major factor in the New Zealand Labor Government's decision to adopt nuclear-free policies that disrupted the ANZUS alliance. In Australia in 1988, an alliance of peace groups and leftists complicated port calls by U.S. Navy ships and prevented a British aircraft carrier from entering Melbourne's harbor. Five years earlier, potential union action triggered an Australian government refusal of dry-dock access to another British carrier in need of repair. Such actions call into question the reliability of U.S. Navy access to Australian ports in the event of any conflict opposed by the Australian left. In the Pacific islands the paucity of their numbers is offset by the inadequacy of counter-balancing political activism.

The extent of direct Soviet involvement in all of the foregoing is difficult to document. The Soviet role in WFTU activities is clear and direct, as are the activities of the Moscow-oriented Australian and New Zealand Marxists. The Soviet Ambassador was expelled from New Zealand in 1980 for financing activities of the Moscow-oriented Socialist Unity Party whose leaders in turn are active in the NZCTU and PTUC. Canberra expelled a Soviet diplomat in 1983 for engaging in similar activities. In August 1987, Australia's then Foreign Minister, Bill Hayden, commented: "There is a surprisingly high level of Soviet-backed activities in South Pacific countries." He went on to say that Australian intelligence reports show that the Soviets are recruiting and funding local activists, primarily through third parties.[16] Beyond these activities, there is a steady flow of regional trade unionists, antinuclear activists, and others to Soviet and Soviet-front sponsored "peace conferences" in Europe and within the region.

Regional Change and Future Prospects

As previously suggested, coincident change in the Pacific islands, change in the Soviet Union, easing of East-West tensions, and related changing

---

[16]Tanham, op. cit., p. 94.

82

threat perceptions together provide new regional opportunities for the Soviets. Other factors offering opportunities for external mischief-makers are increasing political volatility or instability in a number of island states arising from urban drift and massive unemployment, a related erosion of traditional cultural and social restraints, rising economic and social expectations which island governments are ill-equipped to satisfy, discontent with the social and political structures of some states (principally Fiji, Tonga, and Western Samoa), centrifugal separatist forces and an associated rebellion in Papua New Guinea, systematic corruption in the same state, and the potential for a renewal of ethnic communal strife in New Caledonia should there be a breakdown of present arrangements leading to self-determination in 1998.

A further factor is an occasional tendency on the part of some island governments, particularly those of Melanesia, to engage in rhetoric or initiatives designed primarily to demonstrate sovereignty and independence. To some degree this explains Papua New Guinea's decision to accept a Soviet Embassy, and the more recent decision to establish diplomatic relations with Cuba. A potential problem that could exacerbate all of the foregoing is the possibility of the leveling-off or reduction of development assistance from some traditional donors as a consequence of competing domestic pressures and new external priorities, for example, Eastern Europe.

Offsetting the foregoing, most island state governments currently remain essentially conservative and pragmatic, and remarkably cautious about and suspicious of most Soviet motives. With the exception of a very few elites, Soviet ideology remains anathema to the devoutly Christian and fundamentally democratic, free-market oriented island societies. Most island governments also seek to avoid enmeshment in superpower rivalry or competition. The U.S. presence is welcome; there is, in fact, regional pressure for its expansion, and a corollary recognition that expansion of the Soviet presence could lead to increased rivalry with few tangible benefits. Although some island governments may have deliberately played the "Soviet card" to extract higher levels of Western sensitivity and development assistance, by and large they have shown remarkable restraint.

From an island state perspective, the Soviets have little to offer in the way of things tangible other than hard currency payments for fisheries access, possibly modest trade, and, perhaps, marine resource related oceanographic research. However, even with the Soviet Union's meticulous adherence to the terms of its fisheries agreements with Kiribati and Vanuatu, many island states have rejected more recent Soviet offers.

There are also Soviet-origin restraints. The Pacific islands never have been a high priority, so there is a reluctance to apply scarce hard currency to regional objectives. That limitation is exacerbated by the Soviet Union's present economic crisis, and also by the distractions of internal change and turmoil. But even without these restraints, major political or military adventurism within the region would be counterproductive vis-a-vis previously cited higher priority strategic and political objectives. In the more distant future, with a sufficient warming of East-West relations, and with a higher level of Soviet integration into Asia/Pacific political and economic processes, Moscow may be tempted to seek occasional "good will" port calls by naval ships.

At this point it can be argued that direct pursuit of Soviet objectives in the Pacific islands has been marked more by failure than by success. The Soviets thus far have offered little in the way of aid or trade of interest to the region, have failed to win over any government, and continue to have a lower level of presence, dialogue and influence than in any other global region. Such gains as have been made, for example, two aborted fisheries agreements and the establishment of an embassy in Port Moresby, must be measured against the recent zero base. Most political gains, for instance, those involving regional nuclear concerns, can be attributed more to indigenous concerns and Australian and New Zealand leftists and peace groups than to Soviet diplomacy or ideology. Whatever the causes, the effects can be the same—and the Soviets have been efficient in manipulating regional surrogates and others who, for independent reasons, pursue Soviet objectives.

Occasional Western inattention to regional concerns, and policies in conflict with those of regional states, also have been a major factor in Soviet successes to date, for example, the fisheries imbroglio between the United States and regional states; British, French, and U.S. failure to adhere to the SPNFZ protocols; French nuclear testing, and past French colonial policies. There is no question but that Moscow will continue to seek advantage from the foregoing, and will continue to pursue low-cost and low-risk opportunities to erode Western influence. Above all, there will be continuing encouragement and support for regional forces that pursue objectives congruent with Moscow's.

For the future, it is reasonably safe to assume that the Soviet presence and some degree of related influence will expand modestly—for example, additional regional embassies and fisheries agreements, and perhaps some expansion of trade, but not military access. Soviet offers of scholarships and training will also continue to increase and over time could generate expanded but still small cadres of political elites seeking common cause with the Soviets. At a broader level, some island governments may move closer to nonalignment—but probably not in ways that would put at risk major Western sources of development assistance, investment, and trade.

Western Responses

ANZUS strategic denial of any form of Soviet regional access and influence was essentially successful through the mid-1980s, although first Soviet efforts at regional penetration in the mid-1970s required significant increases in development assistance and diplomatic dialogue, and higher levels of Western sensitivity to regional concerns. In the mid-1980s, Canberra and Wellington counseled Kiribati and Vanuatu against Soviet fisheries agreements. In some measure that lack of success reflected not only island state fiscal desperation, but also resentment of a Western double standard. New Zealand and the United States each have fisheries agreements with the Soviet Union, including provision for shore access. That factor, together with the Soviet track record in Kiribati and Vanuatu, and Australia's subsequent negotiations for a trade arrangement to include Soviet fisheries access, have eroded the credibility of Western counsel. In addition, there is now a reluctant Western acceptance that the Soviets do have regional objectives, for example, access to marine resources and to commercial shipping and trade opportunities, that of themselves need not pose a significant threat—so long as they are not co-mingled with political involvement or other elements of strategic competition. More recently, Washington, Canberra, and Wellington have also accepted, however reluctantly, the presence of a Soviet Embassy in Port Moresby. There has been parallel provision of counsel to the Papua New Guinea government on the problems of coping with a Soviet diplomatic and inevitable intelligence presence.

Australia and New Zealand additionally have initiated a number of other measures intended to cope with expanding Soviet activity, and also that of Libya and other adversaries. Intelligence exchanges and defense cooperation with island governments have been strengthened. Both governments provide aerial surveillance of island state EEZs, primarily to monitor fisheries activities, but also Soviet regional maritime activity.

A further consequence has been new Japanese involvement in the region with the encouragement of Canberra and Washington. Tokyo had been concerned by Soviet regional inroads in the late 1980s. Japan also recognized emerging restraints on the ability of traditional Western donors to satisfy regional development requirements, and the parallel desire of island states to diversify economic linkages. Japan in the past several years thus has become the South Pacific's second largest source of aid (after Australia). Japan already was a major source of investment capital and a major regional trading partner. Tokyo also seeks closer cooperation with and perhaps participation in several regional organizations and in time may acquire significant regional political influence.

France, following a 1988 change of government, recognized that past repressive colonial policies, particularly in New Caledonia, ill-served both

French and broader Western interests—and played into the hands of the Soviets, Libyans, and others. Consequences have included new initiatives to resolve the issue of New Caledonia's future, and to provide higher levels of self-government to French Polynesia. These measures have been endorsed by all regional states. Paris has also expanded its regional development assistance programs and diplomatic efforts to cultivate regional governments. However, the present Socialist Government of Prime Minister Rocard, like its conservative predecessors, continues to assert that French nuclear testing remains non-negotiable—although the frequency of tests has been reduced.

Australia's SPNFZ initiative has had a favorable impact within the region. Although the SPNFZ treaty does not go as far as some island states and all peace groups would like, and the Soviet Union and the People's Republic of China are the only nuclear powers to have adhered to the treaty protocols, there has been a subsequent decline of regional antinuclear pressures directed at U.S. naval access. Parallel successes in global arms limitation agreements, and the prospects for further significant East-West cuts in armaments, also appear to have eroded the membership and influence of regional peace groups.

Countering of pacifist, leftist, and Soviet surrogate activities in the Pacific islands is difficult. In 1982 the AFL-CIO and a number of moderate Australian and New Zealand trade union leaders sought to counter these influences by establishing the Labor Committee for Pacific Affairs. The effort foundered as a consequence of inadequate funding, inept American programming of island trade union leaders visiting the United States, and a successful campaign by Australian and New Zealand leftists to discredit the Committee with allegations (false) of CIA involvement. The Asian-American Free Labor Institute, backed by the AFL-CIO, also opened an office in Suva, Fiji, and offered training and other labor-related programs that were well received in the region. However, that effort also has largely foundered as a consequence of inadequate funding and allegations (false) of CIA backing. Moderate Australian, New Zealand, Israeli, British, Canadian, and other trade unions have played a minor positive role in the region, but the WFTU's free world counterpart, the International Confederation of Free Trade Unions (ICFTU) until the recent past largely ignored the region. In short, according to a key Australian trade unionist, moderate labor forces tended to concede the region to the left through neglect.[17] A positive development has been the ICFTU's recent decision to expand its regional activities, including an effort to establish a new regional union grouping to offset or replace the PTUC.

U.S. Information Agency educational and cultural exchange programs have been strengthened in recent years, in part to counter disinformation about U.S. interests, policies, and activities in the region. These have been

[17] Easson, op. cit.

welcomed by island states, but remain inadequate because of budgetary restraints. The United States in 1988 and 1989 also modestly increased development assistance to South Pacific states, expanded its regional diplomatic presence from four to six embassies, and increased levels of diplomatic and other dialogue with island state governments. Resolution of the issue of Palau's future status, a possibility in 1990, would in some degree eliminate an issue that has served Soviet regional objectives.

In all of the foregoing, the most significant Western response has been a reluctant abandonment of total strategic denial of the Soviets. This is partly a consequence of the acceptance of reality, and partly a factor of changing East-West relations. A Soviet diplomatic, trade, and fisheries presence is now accepted, and the application of strategic denial is limited to continuing efforts to exclude military access, intelligence activities, and political meddling or other mischief-making. Given Australia's regional leadership role, a turning point was Foreign Minister Hayden's 1986 assertion, during a visit to Fiji, that the Commonwealth accepted the proposition that the Soviet Union had legitimate interests in the Pacific islands.[18]

Prime Minister Hawke, Hayden, and the current Minister for Foreign Affairs and Trade, Gareth Evans, have also noted that it is unrealistic to attempt to insulate the South Pacific from all Soviet influences, and that a stance of total opposition to a Soviet regional role would be counterproductive—especially in the face of the "warming" of Australian and other Western relationships with Moscow. These ministers have argued that the positive elements of Gorbachev's new policies should be encouraged and that the Soviet Union should be "drawn into" the Pacific community in the absence of sound evidence of Soviet malevolence. However, there also have been expressions of concern by the same ministers about the Soviet lack of "transparency" with respect to their regional objectives, interests, and activities, and most Australian political leaders remain skeptical about Soviet assurances. The Australian government has put Moscow on notice that only "normal" or "conventional" diplomatic behavior will be tolerated.[19]

U.S. officials have been far more reserved. While no longer automatically opposing Soviet regional initiatives, a senior official in mid-1989 observed that "in this era of easing international tensions we hope that Soviet behavior in the Pacific islands will be responsible."[20]

---

[18]"Australia-South Pacific Relations," *Australian Foreign Affairs Record*, Department of Foreign Affairs and Trade, Canberra, Australia, May 1986, pp. 384-385.

[19]I am indebted to Hegarty, op. cit., pp. 122-123, for commentary on Australian and New Zealand reactions to the Soviet presence.

[20]Statement of Acting Deputy Assistant Secretary of State Richard Williams, in U.S. Congress, House, Committee on Foreign Affairs, *Hearing on U.S. Interests in the South Pacific before the Subcommittee on Asian and Pacific Affairs*, 101st Congress, lst Session, July 27, 1989, p. 4.

The New Zealand Labor Government views the emerging Soviet regional presence in much the same fashion as Canberra, but has been more cautious in its public statements—perhaps in part to limit the damage to U.S.-New Zealand relationships already occasioned by New Zealand's disruption of the ANZUS alliance.

The People's Republic of China: Regional Interests and Objectives

The first serious PRC interest in the Pacific islands emerged with regional decolonization in the 1970s and was spurred by concern for Soviet regional initiatives of that period. Like the Soviet Union, China started from a zero regional base, with the exception of the presence of small but affluent Chinese communities in the region's major urban centers. In contrast to the ANZUS powers' application of strategic denial to Soviet efforts to establish a regional presence, there was little or no Western resistance to PRC embassies within the region, other political initiatives, and establishment of regional aid programs. Beijing's regional diplomacy generally has been perceived as reinforcing Western efforts to exclude the Soviets.

As with the Soviets, Chinese regional objectives relate less to intrinsic regional interests than to broader strategic and political considerations, with the exception of sporadic limited interest in the region's marine resources. In particular, there has been concern for Soviet "hegemonic" encirclement of China and for the possibility that Soviet regional successes could erode counter-balancing Western influence and military strength. Other objectives relate to Taiwan's regional presence and "Third World solidarity." In that context, the following pattern of PRC objectives and regional policy themes emerged in the mid-1970s and have been constant in the 1980s:

• Establishment of diplomatic relations with the region's island states.

• Demonstration of "Third World solidarity," including the establishment of a diplomatic presence essential for Beijing's global and regional influence objectives.

• Blocking of Soviet diplomatic and other regional access.

• Diplomatic support for the ANZUS alliance, including subtle support for the encouragement of a Western military presence as a counter to Soviet military and "hegemonic" threats.

• Displacement or blocking of Taiwan's diplomatic and economic relationships.

• Establishment of small but highly visible and popular aid programs intended to yield political influence.

The Emerging Chinese Presence

An essential pre-condition to Western and island state acceptance of a PRC regional presence was met in the early 1970s by Australia's and New Zealand's establishment of diplomatic relations with Beijing, and President Nixon's China initiative leading to restored Chinese-American relationships. Chinese diplomatic relations with Fiji and Western Samoa followed in 1975 , with Papua New Guinea in 1976, and with other regional states in the 1980s. Embassies were established in Fiji, Western Samoa, and Papua New Guinea. (Though low profile, the Chinese diplomatic presence in the South Pacific was in fact greater than that of the United States until 1988.) These developments were generally coincident and deliberate parallels to early Soviet regional diplomatic initiatives.

Aid, technical assistance, cultural exchanges, and reciprocal high-level official visits followed. Sports stadiums were constructed in Western Samoa and Papua New Guinea, as well as the parliament house in Vanuatu. There have also been multimillion-dollar interest-free loans and cash grants to key island states (particularly Fiji), trade agreements (e.g., purchase of Fiji sugar), and multiple technical assistance and training programs, some involving university scholarships and other programs in China. Following Fiji's 1987 military coups, China provided medical teams to offset the loss of emigrating Indo-Fijian medical specialists.

There also have been official visits to Beijing by regional prime ministers, foreign ministers, and other cabinet-level officials, and reciprocal Chinese visits. The most notable of the latter was the 1985 regional tour of then Communist Party General Secretary Hu Yaobang who counseled his hosts on the perils of Soviet "hegemonism." The anti-Soviet comments of then Chinese Vice Premier Li Hsien-Nien at a 1978 Beijing banquet honoring the visit of Fiji's Prime Minister, Ratu Sir Kamisese Mara, were sufficiently pointed to prompt a walk-out by Soviet bloc diplomatic guests. [21]

Commitment to "Third World solidarity" did prompt Beijing's early adherence to the SPNFZ Treaty of Rarotonga protocols, but apparently with some misgivings. One influential Chinese scholar has cautioned that measures such as SPNFZ have the potential to affect negatively Chinese security interests since a "neutral Pacific is a Soviet Pacific."[22] Beijing also has been unsympathetic to New Zealand's disruption of the ANZUS alliance, and has counseled island state governments against adoption of "nuclear-free" policies paralleling those of Wellington.

Beijing has been less than successful in its efforts to displace or block Taiwan's presence. Four smaller island states, Nauru, the Solomons,

---

[21] John Hoffman, "Second Walkout by Soviet Bloc Envoys," *Sydney Morning Herald*, June 13, 1978, p. 32.

[22] Hua Di, "The Soviet Threat to the Northern Pacific Region from an Overall Point of View," *Atlantic Community Quarterly*, Vol. XXIV, Spring 1986, pp. 145-149.

Tonga, and Tuvalu, maintain diplomatic or consular relationships with Taiwan, and quasi-official Taiwan trade offices have been established in some other states, including Papua New Guinea and Fiji. Several island states, for example, the Marshall Islands, have been receptive to Taiwan's offers of aid and joint economic ventures.

The regional images of both Taipei and Beijing have suffered in the past several years for unrelated reasons. Taiwan's fishing fleets too frequently have poached tuna from island state EEZs, and have engendered regional outrage by engaging (as do the Japanese) in drift-net fishing—a technology that has been likened to marine-life strip-mining. Beijing in turn has suffered from regional reaction to the violent repression of the Chinese democracy movement.

Future Prospects

Beijing probably will continue to maintain a low-profile presence in the Pacific islands. Although there has been some improvement in Soviet-Chinese relations, for the foreseeable future there can be little doubt that Beijing will continue low-key efforts to counter Soviet regional political .initiatives. However, China's limited influence may wane further as a consequence of Taiwan's inroads, unfavorable regional comparisons of Soviet internal reform vis-a-vis Chinese domestic repression, regional perceptions of a decreasing Soviet threat, and new economic restraints on Beijing's ability to offer significant regional aid or trade arrangements.

By way of contrast, Taiwan's enormous foreign exchange reserves and related expanding technical and development assistance programs—and a willingness to use these assets in the pursuit of political objectives—suggest that Taiwan's presence may increase, especially in smaller states that are particularly aid-dependent.

From a Western perspective, the Chinese presence in the Pacific islands—Beijing's and Taipei's—has generally been a political plus and probably will remain so.

Conclusions

Glasnost, perestroika, democratization processes in Eastern Europe, change and turmoil in the Soviet Union, and improving East-West relations are all reality—but so is uncertainty about the durability of Soviet reform and its ultimate impact on traditional Soviet strategic and political objectives. At best, it can be assumed that the Soviet Union will remain the West's most formidable political competitor and, even with the receding threat of global conflict, its most dangerous potential military adversary. Beyond these considerations, there is as yet no evidence of any change in Soviet objectives relating to erosion of Western military access to and influence in the Pacific islands. Australian expert David Hegarty has pointed out that, equally, there is no evidence that the Soviet Union has abandoned its extra-diplomatic methods of political penetration and manipulation through use of "non-political" activities such as trade, aid, scientific, cultural, and sporting links.[23] In a major policy statement in December 1989, Australian Foreign Minister Gareth Evans summed it up well: "In the South Pacific, we should expect continued manifestations (for the most part opportunistic) of Soviet attempts to gain influence and supporters and to erode the strong pro-Western bias of the region, particularly since the investment of relatively small resources can yield disproportionate results."[24]

The Pacific islands do remain a relatively low priority for the Soviet Union, although the level of Moscow's interest and activity in the region has significantly increased in recent years as a consequence of broader East-West and Asia/Pacific strategies, and of the region's relationship to these areas of higher priority. There also is the long-standing interest in the region's rich tuna resource and the potential for seabed mining. These developments have been paralleled by far more sophisticated regional diplomacy which has had some early limited successes. The prospect is for more of the latter—but probably not to the point of being a catalyst for fundamental regional realignments. To the extent that Western influence and interests within the Pacific islands may suffer erosion in the future, this is more likely to be a consequence of indigenous regional change, Western inattention or policies and actions inconsistent with regional state concerns, and the activities of Soviet surrogates or others pursuing objectives congruent with Moscow's.

None of the foregoing is intended to suggest that there is no direct Soviet strategic or political threat. It does mean that exaggerating the threat, and blaming Moscow for most indigenous challenges to Western interests, ignores reality and assures flawed responses. Clearly, however, Western states with major regional interests, and the regional states themselves, must monitor Soviet activities—and develop stronger multilateral consultative and policy coordination mechanisms. At a minimum, these processes must involve Australia, France, Japan, New Zealand, and the United States, and must assure high levels of political sensitivity to regional concerns. Equally, development assistance levels essential to the region's political stability must continue. The Western strategy of deterrence of conflict through alliance strength and cooperation also will remain essential

---

[23]Hegarty, op. cit., p. 120.

[24]"Australia's Regional Security," ministerial statement of Senator Gareth Evans, Minister for Foreign Affairs and Trade, Canberra, Australia, December 6, 1989, p. 5.

in the Pacific as elsewhere, although hopefully at lower and less threatening armament levels.

Beyond governmental responses to the Soviets and their regional initiatives, there is a role for the private sector. All island states prefer private investment and export trade opportunities to aid-handouts, and there are opportunities in this area. At the political level, moderate trade unions in Western states with regional interests could do more to offset the activities of the WFTU and regional leftists—as should the ICFTU.

From a Western perspective, change and challenge in the Pacific islands, including Soviet and other new external influences, have not yet reached unmanageable proportions, especially since regional state and Western strategic interests generally remain compatible. In that context, a major challenge for the West will be to develop a political strategy for the Pacific, including dialogue with the Soviets, which will channel the latter's new presence in directions that mesh with broader strategies intended ultimately to integrate the Soviet Union into the matrix of normal global political and economic processes.

As to Beijing and Taipei, their mutual competition serves some regional state interests by offering alternative external linkages and the benefits of competing aid and trade offers. From a Western perspective, Beijing's continuing opposition to a Soviet regional presence and support of counter-balancing Western regional security requirements does serve U.S. and allied strategic interests. However, the political influence of both Chinas within the region is likely to remain marginal. There is little or no reason for Western states to attempt to interfere in regional Beijing-Taipei competition. However, shared PRC and Western strategic interests relative to the Soviet Union in the Pacific islands do warrant consultations between regionally-involved Western states and Beijing.

U.S. Policy toward the South Pacific

by L. R. Vasey and Robert L. Pfaltzgraff, Jr.

With the emergence of the Pacific rim as an area of dynamic growth and change, the vast "in-between" region encompassing the Pacific islands has grown in importance—as have Australia's and New Zealand's roles in and relationships with that region. Scattered over some 88 million square kilometers of the Pacific Ocean, the islands embrace thirteen states and eight dependent territories, but have a land area less than that of Texas, and a population of only 5.9 million. Not counting Papua New Guinea's 3.6 million inhabitants, average populations are about 100,000. Most island states are handicapped by few natural resources, scarce and infertile land, and the continual threat of natural disaster. Only Papua New Guinea and Fiji (discounting self-sufficient phosphate-rich but minuscule Nauru), and possibly the Solomons and Vanuatu, appear to have a resource base offering hope of future economic self-sufficiency. Most other states or territories are likely to be permanently aid-dependent. Nevertheless, the region's political life, at least until the recent past, has been stable and largely free of discord. Democratic institutions emerged in most states and the region's human rights record is without parallel elsewhere in the Third World. Nearly all island state governments have a pro-West orientation; only one (Vanuatu) has joined the nonaligned movement, although others may follow.

Until the 1960s all of the islands were colonies, UN trust territories, or protectorates of external powers: Australia, Britain, France, New Zealand, and the United States. Thereafter, progress toward independence or self-government was rapid for a majority of them (French territories being a conspicuous exception), but vestiges of the colonial era have generated political crises in some areas. In Fiji, for example, nearly half of the population is Indian—descendants of indentured labor imported by Britain to work the sugar plantations of those islands. That demography prompted two military coups in 1987 by ethnic Fijians determined to institutionalize ethnic Fijian political control of their island nation. In New Caledonia, still a French territory, a mix of Vietnamese, Polynesians from other islands, and French settlers (mainly the latter) have become the majority. Indigenous Melanesian "Kanak" demands for independence and resultant conflict in the recent past have prompted levels of violence amounting to insurrection in that troubled territory.

Close American bonds to the region were forged in World War II when the strategic importance of the islands became apparent in the "stepping-stone" battles of the Pacific war. They provided staging bases for Japanese advances toward Australia and Hawaii, and then for the allies in the campaigns leading to Japan's defeat. Although the American military presence in the islands was overwhelming, it also left an enormous reservoir of goodwill toward the United States. What seemed to have most impressed Pacific islanders was the perception of egalitarian attitudes of American servicemen toward them in contrast to the often cavalier treat-ment by colonial administrators and planters. A notable legacy of the Pacific War was the infusion of the physical infrastructure still present throughout the region in the form of harbors, airports, and roads con-structed by American engineers. Some major airports still bear American names. However, U.S. inattention to the newly independent South Pacific states and perceived insensitivity toward their concerns and interests resulted in considerable depletion of that reservoir of goodwill in the 1970s and throughout most of the 1980s.

With the conclusion of the Pacific war, the American presence in the Pacific islands was for the most part terminated, except in the U.S. territories (Guam and American Samoa), and the Northern Mariana, Caroline, and Marshall islands. Formerly controlled by Japan, these North Pacific Micronesian island groups came under U.S. administration as the UN Trust Territory of the Pacific Islands—but with a commitment to their peoples and to the United Nations to develop them toward "self-government or inde-pendence." In the decades following the Pacific war, Washington's priorities shifted to commitments and issues in other parts of the globe. The development of the South Pacific was left largely in the hands of Australia, New Zealand, France, and Britain. However, the latter's withdrawal from the region was virtually complete by 1980 following decolonization of Britain's Pacific possessions. The American diplomatic presence in the South Pacific was negligible, and U.S. bilateral develop-ment assistance to that region was non-existent prior to the late 1970s. The single major security development was the conclusion in 1951 of the ANZUS pact between Australia, New Zealand, and the United States. ANZUS provided a security umbrella over the region, and a framework for political cooperation related to shared strategic and political interests.

As decolonization progressed, an informal division of labor emerged between the ANZUS partners: the United States focused on its areas of influence and presence in the North Pacific islands, while Australia and New Zealand focused on the South Pacific. The basic strategic concern

94

of all three partners, as pointed out by Robert Kiste,[1] was to assure the region remained under Western influence, and that a Soviet military or political presence was excluded. The latter objective, "strategic denial," was to foreclose the possibility of the islands ever again being used by an adversary to interdict critical Pacific air and sea lanes of communication.

Economic Development and Socio-Political Change

Two major trends are likely to have a definitive influence on the future of the Pacific islands: the course of economic development, and socio-political change flowing from modernization processes, shifts in demography, new external influences, and generational leadership change. As previously indicated, all island states and territories have narrowly-based economies. With the exception of Fiji and minuscule Nauru, all are heavily dependent on external development assistance and budget support grants for maintenance of even minimal levels of services and physical infrastructure essential to the welfare of their peoples and thus for political stability. (France's major military presence in its territories, its nuclear-testing program in French Polynesia, and the U.S. military presence in Guam and the Marshall Islands provide additional important revenue for these areas.) With few exceptions, aid dependency is actually increasing while external assistance levels and GDP growth rates are either static or in decline.

All island states seek higher levels of foreign investment—including investment from the United States—and new markets for their products. However, with some major exceptions, the potential for private sector foreign investment is limited, and even then not adequately developed. The same applies to limited possibilities in the area of export trade development. A further problem is that of unplanned urbanization, and accompanying high levels of unemployment and crime. These developments are eroding traditional cultures and their social discipline restraints with uncertain consequences for the region's future stability.

In the area of economic assistance, the United States has been generous with its Pacific territories and the Micronesian states in free association with it—nearly $400 million in 1988. But these areas represent only about 5 percent of the region's population. For the balance, the independent states of the South Pacific, U.S. aid levels remain minuscule, although increased from a past pattern of about $4-6 million annually to $22 million

---

[1] Henry S. Albinski et al., *The South Pacific: Political, Economic, and Military Trends* (Washington, D.C.: Brassey's [US], Inc., for the Pacific Forum/CSIS and the Institute for Foreign Policy Analysis, 1989). Robert C. Kiste's paper is entitled "The Island States as Actors in the Region," pp. 27-44.

in 1988. Even at that level, U.S. development assistance to the South Pacific is less than 4 percent of total flows, and lags well behind that of Australia, Japan, New Zealand, France, Britain, and the European Community. Low levels of U.S. assistance have generated islander perceptions of American insensitivity to regional needs, and a belief that Washington has not adequately reciprocated island state support for U.S. interests and policies.

There are no easy answers to the questions of how much and what type of assistance will suffice with respect to either regional development requirements and expectations, or maintenance of U.S. interests. Clearly the United States cannot match the high levels of aid from traditional South Pacific donors (e.g., Australia's approximately $300 million annually). Nor would it be appropriate (or possible) to attempt to supplant Australia's and New Zealand's traditional roles and influence. However, U.S. South Pacific interests and regional need do argue for modest increases, particularly in those areas where the United States has an obvious comparative advantage, such as managerial training and entrepreneurial skills. Projects accenting human resource development and private sector export-oriented commercial potential (e.g., fisheries), and that identify with island state economic goals could yield impressive dividends at relatively small cost to the United States. Of equal or greater long-term value would be programs providing encouragement to American private sector investment, and "free trade" access to U.S. markets for island products. Precedents for the latter exist in the Caribbean, and in Australia's and New Zealand's SPARTECA Pacific islands free trade regime.

Changes taking place in the basic structures of island societies are likely to contribute to increasing political volatility or instability in some areas. In spite of high levels of emigration from some of the smaller Polynesian states, future island populations will be larger, younger, and increasingly urban. More than 50 percent of the region's population is 16 or younger. Generational change throughout the Pacific islands is resulting in a new leadership more nationalistic, in some cases inclined to question traditional Western linkages, influence, and values, and prone to experiment with new international linkages. The consequence in some states already has been a reassessment and realignment of foreign policy priorities—including reinforcement and expansion of economic relationships in an ongoing search for economic security, or at least diversification of aid dependency. New links with the Soviet Union, the ASEAN states, Japan, Taiwan, the People's Republic of China, and even Libya have been among the positive and negative consequences.

Regionalism and Regional Organizations

Other South Pacific trends also hold important implications for U.S. interests. Regional organizations, as Richard Herr observes,[2] are becoming a more influential regional force. Regionalism in fact has been an important factor since the creation of the South Pacific Commission (SPC) in 1947. More recently the South Pacific Forum (SPF), established in 1971, has served as a primary mechanism for establishment of regional positions on decolonization, nuclear and other environmental concerns, fisheries management, and so on. Regional economic organizations, such as the SPF's Secretariat (formerly the South Pacific Bureau for Economic Cooperation), the Forum Fisheries Agency, the Committee for Coordination of Joint Prospecting for Mineral Resources in South Pacific Offshore Areas, acting under the aegis of either the SPC or SPF, are expanding in number. The objectives of these organizations include promotion and coordination of development and technical assistance to the region, development and promotion of private investment opportunities and export markets, and management and conservation of marine resources. They also provide economies of scale to the region's mini-states, often assuming the functions normally performed by larger states elsewhere. These organizations in some cases are the primary interface between smaller island states and the broader global community.

The Forum, whose membership embraces all of the region's independent and self-governing states, plus Australia and New Zealand, has outstripped the Commission as the region's unified voice. In 1989 it initiated, on the pattern of the ASEAN post-ministerial meetings, an annual post-Forum "dialogue" with key non-members having a regional presence or other regional interests: Britain, Canada, France, Japan, and the United States. China was invited but did not participate in 1989. The Soviet Union was not invited, but that may happen in the future; Soviet participation would give Moscow unprecedented regional political access.

Disintegrative and Destabilizing Forces

The trend toward regionalism is being countered to some extent by disintegrative forces. Ethnic divisions, particularly between Melanesia and Polynesia, are likely to deepen as cultural awareness increases. Such trends may be reinforced by the dramatic differences in land masses and populations between the Melanesian states on the one hand, and the micro-states of Polynesia and Micronesia on the other. The Melanesian states have already formed the "Melanesian Spearhead Group," a move that may in time prompt a similar organizational response from Polynesia

---

2 Richard Herr, "Future Roles of Regional Organizations: Implications for Policy," in ibid., pp. 45-62.

and, perhaps, from Micronesia. In turn, these disintegrative forces have the potential to erode the effectiveness of regional organizations, including the role they have played in assuring moderation in regional approaches to regional concerns and issues. The latter factor alone requires U.S. monitoring of these trends as an element of a broader strategy to encourage regionalism as a force for regional development and stability. As a non-member of most regional organizations, the United States (unlike Australia and New Zealand) has little direct influence. However, it can and should give more serious attention and support to the few organizations to which it belongs—principally the SPC—by assuring higher levels of and more expert U.S. representation.

Other major forces for instability within the region include the previously mentioned ethnic divisions in Fiji which prompted coups in that state and the destruction of its democratic institutions, the clash between French settlers and indigenous Kanaks in New Caledonia over the political future of that French territory, and centrifugal forces in Papua New Guinea which have already prompted a secessionist rebellion in that state. The United States has little or no ability to influence directly these and other troublesome internal political problems, but can and should work with other Western powers that do have influence in these areas—especially Australia, New Zealand, and France. For the longer term, higher levels of development assistance that can help to provide the levels of economic security essential to political stability can also be a most effective American strategy—and would also provide higher levels of political influence than exist at present.

With the exception of Papua New Guinea, which for over 20 years has experienced occasional Indonesian military forays across a common land border—forays conducted not against Papua New Guinea, but against West Irian insurrectionists operating along the border—no island state perceives any external military threat, except in the context of an unlikely global or broader regional conflict. For that reason few states maintain military forces, and most have perceived ANZUS as providing such security as may be required for the region. Those that do have military or paramilitary forces (Papua New Guinea, Fiji, Tonga, and Vanuatu) keep them primarily for internal security purposes. There is little perceived need, support, or prospect for a regional security arrangement.

Defense Cooperation

The United States has developed small but welcome defense cooperation programs with Papua New Guinea, Fiji, and Tonga, although that with Fiji was terminated following the 1987 coups. Although there may be scope for some expansion of U.S. defense cooperation in the South Pacific, it will be important not to compete with or disrupt long-standing and broader linkages between South Pacific states and Australia and New Zealand.

The United States also has responsibility for the defense of the Micronesian states in the North Pacific that are in free association with it. U.S. military "civic action" teams additionally have played a minor but welcome role in island state public works projects, and also have provided major disaster relief following hurricanes.

In the South Pacific, Australia and New Zealand have developed close defense links and commitments to most island states—a region of vital strategic significance to each nation. Canberra and Wellington also accept the possibility of an island state internal crisis requiring their armed intervention, if only to provide support to a friendly government under domestic siege, or to evacuate their nationals.

In contrast to the island states' focus on economic security, the United States, Australia, and New Zealand—as well as Japan and other East Asian allies and friends—attach high strategic importance to the region. The island states and territories straddle or are proximate to the air and sea lanes of communication that link the rim nations; these lanes carry nearly one-half of all American foreign trade, and connect the United States to five of its seven alliance relationships. Preservation of freedom of navigation and the security of these trans-Pacific routes thus is a vital national interest for nearly all the Pacific rim nations—but also for island states dependent on export-import trade.

Regional Issues

Marine Resources. Although there are numerous shared or compatible interests, some activities of external powers, principally the United States, France, Japan, and Taiwan, at times have been seen as threatening by island states. As one example, for ten years through the mid-1980s, the American Tuna Boat Association was accused of "poaching" the tuna resource of island state exclusive economic zones. As Henry S. Albinski has noted,[3] resource-poor and economically distressed island states bitterly resented and criticized the United States for its slowness in taking corrective action to resolve jurisdictional legal disputes. The fishing controversy also eroded U.S. efforts to block Soviet regional access. Although a 1987 fisheries convention resolved the issue, and provided generous financial terms in return for U.S. fisheries access, the problem already had reinforced an existing perception of American insensitivity to regional concerns. More recently, Japanese and Taiwanese drift-net fishing has been seen as a serious threat to the region's marine resources, and has prompted regional state outrage. Continued French nuclear testing is also

---

[3] Henry S. Albinski, "South Pacific Trends and U.S. Security Implications: An Introductory Overview," in ibid., pp. 1-26.

perceived as a threat to the region's environment, particularly marine resources.

Environment. Related to the latter point, a major regional concern has been that of environmental pollution. Pacific island peoples rely heavily on the sea for food, while the foreign exchange earnings of many states are dependent upon the rich tuna resource of their surrounding exclusive economic zones. The seas also are a major element in the vital tourist trade. For these reasons the South Pacific Regional Environmental Programme (SPREP) was formulated to protect the marine environment against pollution from land-based sources, harmful seabed activities, and hazardous waste disposal; it does not address the issue of nuclear testing. The United States has adhered to the SPREP convention.

French Policies. France has long been under pressure to grant independence to New Caledonia, but conservative governments in Paris pursued repressive policies in that territory while viewing pressures for change from the region as an Anglo-Saxon manipulated conspiracy to displace the French presence. The United States, caught between its vital interests in Europe and regional interests in the South Pacific, sought to remain disengaged and limited itself to vaguely worded expressions of support for the principle of self-determination. The net result was a regional impression of tacit support for the French position. Following renewal of violence in New Caledonia, the newly elected Socialist Rocard Government in Paris in 1988 crafted with all parties in New Caledonia an accord that provides for major political, economic, and social development programs leading to an act of self-determination in 1998.

All regional governments and the United States have endorsed the above accord, but there is concern that extremists, either indigenous Kanak or French settler, may attempt to sabotage it. (Indeed, in 1989 Kanak extremists assassinated the moderate leader of the Kanak independence movement.) Similar problems could emerge in French Polynesia, France's nuclear test site, where a majority seeks higher levels of self-government and a potentially violent minority favors independence.

In all of this, there is the potential for conflict between U.S. regional interests and traditional support for the principle of self-determination on the one hand, and traditionally important links with France on the other. The best outcome, from U.S., Australian, New Zealand, and island state perspectives, would include (a) an independent New Caledonia with continuing close relationships with France; (b) a self-governing French Polynesia (perhaps a form of free association similar to that of the Micronesian states with the United States) with close links to France; and (c) a continuing French presence through development assistance, participation in the South Pacific Commission and other regional institutions, and stabilizing political ties with its former territories.

U.S. Strategic Interests. For the United States, the evolution of the Trust Territory of the Pacific Islands to self-determination and self-government has been relatively smooth, with one exception. The Northern Mariana Islands have entered into a commonwealth relationship with the United States following a UN-observed act of self-determination. The Marshall Islands and the Federated States of Micronesia have each entered into a free association relationship as sovereign, self-governing states responsible for their internal and foreign affairs, but with defense responsibility delegated to the United States. Either state can unilaterally terminate the relationship in favor of full independence. Palau, the last remaining element of the Trust Territory, in seven acts of self-determination over seven years, also has opted for free association, but always with a majority less than the 75 percent mandated by its constitution. That unique majority is necessary to override constitutional "nuclear-free" provisions that are in conflict with the free association arrangement's delegation of defense authority to the United States. (In a free association relationship, U.S. ships and aircraft, some potentially nuclear-armed, would have access to Palau's ports and airfields and would be governed by the U.S. policy of neither confirming nor denying the presence of nuclear weaponry.)

A political alternative to free association might be independence for Palau, but also a close treaty relationship with the United States which protects fundamental U.S. security interests, for example, exclusion of any third party military presence. The failure of the last referendum on free association (February 6, 1990) to achieve the mandated 75 percent approval may make this option more attractive. However, Palau's "nuclear-free" constitutional provisions probably would apply, with the consequence that limited U.S. military options in Palau could be further severely inhibited.

Meanwhile, the Soviets, leftists in the Pacific area, and various "peace groups" have portrayed the United States as an imperialist power attempting to impose free association on Palau so that it might place "nuclear bases" in those islands. The allegations are ironic in that there are no restraints on U.S. military activity in Palau so long as it remains a trust territory; on the other hand, stationing or storage of nuclear weapons is prohibited by the free association agreement with Palau. Nonetheless, the allegations are widely believed, and continuing delay in resolving Palau's future status has become a major political and diplomatic embarrassment.

There are no significant internal or external pressures for "decolonization" of the U.S. territories of Guam and American Samoa. Both wish to retain close political links with the United States. However, the former seeks commonwealth status and higher levels of self-government, and similar pressures may emerge in the future in American Samoa.

All of the above areas of U.S. presence or influence, with the possible exception of American Samoa, are of actual or potential strategic significance. The Kwajalein Missile Range Facility in the Marshall Islands will remain essential so long as there is a need to test ICBMs. It also is a critical element in the ongoing development of the Strategic Defense Initiative. The same facility and one in the Northern Mariana Islands are also part of a major space-tracking system essential to the detection of Soviet satellite launches. Guam's air and naval facilities are an important element in the deployment of U.S. forces in the Western Pacific. In the event of loss of access to facilities in the Philippines, some operations could be transferred there, and to Palau and to Saipan and Tinian in the Northern Marianas. However, political restraints, cost factors, the absence of large and skilled work forces, and land-mass restraints preclude transfer of most major operations, for example, those of Subic Bay.

Denuclearizaton. Nuclear issues, as Ramesh Thakur points out,[4] are a major regional political concern. With the termination of American and British nuclear testing in the Pacific in the early 1960s, French testing (begun in the mid-1960s) has become the catalyst for antinuclear sentiment throughout the South Pacific. The region has been united, vocal, and persistent in its opposition to that testing—and probably will remain so. The 1985 bombing and sinking in Auckland harbor of the Greenpeace ship *Rainbow Warrior* by French intelligence agents gave new focus to regional outrage. France, in response, continues to assert that its requirement for nuclear testing in French Polynesia remains non-negotiable, although it has (since election of the Rocard Government in 1988) demonstrated new flexibility and sensitivity with respect to other issues—particularly those of the future political status of French territories.

The 1985 Treaty of Rarotonga, which established the South Pacific Nuclear Free Zone (SPNFZ), is aimed primarily at French nuclear testing, and was an Australian initiative intended to contain pressures for a more extreme arrangement which would have inhibited regional access by nuclear-armed or -powered ships. The treaty thus was crafted to assure consistency with U.S. regional security interests and criteria for adherence to nuclear-weapons free zones. Stationing and storage of nuclear weaponry within the zone are prohibited, but there is no U.S. requirement for such. All nuclear powers were invited to respect the provisions of the SPNFZ by adhering to treaty protocols. The Soviet Union and the PRC have adhered. France refused since such action would require a close-down of its Pacific nuclear-test site. Britain and the United States have publicly affirmed that SPNFZ does not conflict with their regional security interests and requirements, but declined to adhere on the basis that such action could promote higher levels of pressure for nuclear-weapons free zones in other areas (e.g., Southeast Asia) where there would be significant damage to Western security interests. The American decision was deeply resented in the region, particularly because of the regional effort to defer to U.S. criteria

---

[4] See above, pp. 27-51.

for adherence. The Soviets have with some success exploited the U.S. position and its contrast to that of Moscow's adherence.

Australia and New Zealand

In the final analysis, U.S. security interests in the South Pacific, except for its special relationship with Australia, are modest compared to those in the North Pacific and elsewhere in the world. No military bases are sought or required, although port access is important for the U.S. Navy—as is continued denial of military access by potential adversaries. On the other hand, the South Pacific is of major strategic importance to Australia and New Zealand, if only because it dominates the strategic approaches to both nations.

In the above circumstances it remains appropriate that these two nations continue to play the lead Western role in the South Pacific where they are accepted as political, economic, and security partners. However, the supportive secondary role of the United States in the South Pacific is becoming of increasing importance as new challenges to U.S. and other Western interests emerge in that area. This requires higher levels of diplomatic presence and dialogue, greater sensitivity toward regional concerns, and higher levels of U.S. development assistance.

Until the mid-1980s, the United States, Australia, and New Zealand, with their closely allied interests and values, found it relatively easy to pursue a regional order based on shared objectives. Since then, divergent concerns and issues have arisen which have threatened or eroded the harmony and effectiveness of that ANZUS arrangement.

The Australian-American relationship, according to Ross Babbage,[5] remains resilient, in spite of increasing nationalist sentiment and an emerging perception among Australians that the alliance relationship benefits the United States more than Australia. Agricultural trade issues also have troubled the relationship. Nonetheless, Australia remains a staunch and important ally in both a regional and global context. Australian-American "joint defense facilities" in Australia, mainly satellite ground stations, are vital elements of Western defense and critical to arms control agreements. They provide verification of the latter, detection of Soviet missile launches, and sophisticated intelligence collection capabilities. One facility is also important for Australian and American communication with submerged submarines. U.S. Navy access to Australian ports is essential to naval operations in the South Pacific and much of the Indian Ocean. Although Australian defense planning now focuses on self-sufficiency with respect to regional threats, continuing close cooperation between Australian and

---

[5] Ross Babbage, "Australian Interests in the South Pacific," in Albinski, op. cit., pp. 63-83.

U.S. forces assures a capability for joint operations in a broader conflict. Australian military assets would be essential in any conflict threatening sea lanes in the South Pacific, or in much of the Indian Ocean.

As the South Pacific's superpower, Australia is the major force for stability and security in the region, and the major source of development assistance. Yet its pervasive presence and influence in some degree is also a concern for smaller states sensitive about their sovereignty and freedom of political action. Australia, in developing its own regional policies, thus takes into account island state concerns, which in turn bring it into conflict with U.S. and French regional policies or actions—for example, with the United States over regional fisheries practices (prior to resolution of this issue in 1987) and the establishment of SPNFZ, and with France over nuclear testing, SPNFZ, and French policy in New Caledonia prior to 1988. Australia also has pressed the United States to strengthen its diplomatic presence in and dialogue with the island states, increase development assistance, and play a more active role in the South Pacific Commission.

In contrast to the close and effective Australian-American alliance, the 1984 election in New Zealand of a Labor Government committed to a "nuclear-free" New Zealand brought on the 1985 disruption of the American-New Zealand leg of the ANZUS relationship. New Zealand's ban from its ports and waters of nuclear-armed or nuclear-propelled ships in effect banned the U.S. Navy. The United States responded by suspending its alliance commitments to New Zealand, terminating defense cooperation, and placing restraints on diplomatic dialogue. Antinuclear sentiment is deeply rooted in New Zealand, and most New Zealanders (unlike Australians) perceive few if any potential threats to their security. Some observers perceive a New Zealand drift toward pacifism and isolationism.

Nonetheless, New Zealand's objectives in the South Pacific generally still parallel those of Australia and the United States: promotion of political stability and democratic institutions, support for regionalism and regional institutions, exclusion of unfriendly external influences, and support for the economic development essential to economic security and thus political stability. Denis McLean also argues that isolationist tendencies in New Zealand should not be exaggerated.[6] Political, cultural, and economic ties with the Western world remain strong, and may be strengthened as New Zealand's commerce expands; she remains heavily dependent on the export of agricultural products. However, New Zealand is expanding its export trade with the European Community, Japan, and other Pacific basin states in Asia and South America, a trend that in time may provide more political flexibility by lessening its current heavy reliance on U.S. markets.

---

[6]Dennis McLean, "Perspectives from New Zealand: Interests, Objectives, Means, and Prospects," in ibid., pp. 84-100.

Among the extra-regional powers attempting to increase their presence in the Pacific islands, the Soviet Union remains potentially the most threatening with respect to Western interests. The fact that the Soviets have not achieved a military lodgment in the area can be attributed in some measure to the ANZUS "strategic denial" policy—but also very much to deeply-rooted suspicion of the Soviets throughout the Pacific islands. For the foreseeable future no island state government is likely to welcome a Soviet military presence. Despite New Zealand's disruption of the ANZUS alliance, Wellington remains united with Canberra and Washington in opposing not only any Soviet military presence, but also any political activity directed at Western regional interests. There is a consequent continuing potential for effective coalition diplomacy.

Soviet Interests and Objectives

Glasnost, perestroika, the ongoing collapse of the Soviet empire, lessening East-West tension, and a decline in the threat of global conflict are all reality. Nonetheless, the Soviet Union will remain the West's primary strategic competitor at a political level, and its most dangerous potential military adversary. Fortunately, however, the Soviet Union's ability to project naval power into the South Pacific is limited by a number of factors, including lack of a basing structure and port access.

Nevertheless, the Soviet Union continues to maintain a formidable Pacific military capability, particularly in the area of submarine warfare. In his July 1986 Vladivostok speech, Gorbachev also asserted that the Asia-Pacific area is of growing strategic importance to the Soviet Union. Thus, if Soviet interest in the Pacific continues to grow, as Gorbachev has suggested, it follows that the South Pacific will also become an arena of increased salience for Soviet policy.

Soviet diplomacy under Gorbachev has assumed a more innovative character in which ideology is given less prominence and emphasis is placed on improving the Soviet Union's political image in the region. According to Jusuf Wanandi and John Dorrance,[7] since 1986 Moscow has pursued Pacific islands policies oriented toward issues of concern to regional states. These include: (a) support for New Caledonia's independence (while the United States appeared indifferent or pro-French); (b) support for the South Pacific Nuclear Free Zone and adherence to the protocols of the Treaty of Rarotonga (while Washington refused to adhere); (c) political and psychological exploitation of U.S. differences with New Zealand over the latter's nuclear-free policies; and (d) advancement of the Soviet concept of "equal economic security assistance." The Soviet Union also has initiated new cultural exchanges, trade union liaison arrangements and training programs, and visits by Pacific islanders to the Soviet Union and

---

[7] See above, pp. 52-65 and 66-92.

Eastern bloc states. The first Soviet diplomatic presence in the Pacific islands will be established in the near future with an embassy in Papua New Guinea. Others may follow.

The Soviet Union has been adroit in seizing opportunities to enhance its regional image and presence. While the United States was embroiled in fisheries disputes with the region, Moscow extended numerous attractive fisheries agreement offers, and concluded two with Kiribati and Vanuatu on terms more generous than proffered by Japan and the United States. Both agreements were terminated after one year, but new offers were made in 1989 to other regional states, principally Papua New Guinea. There also have been offers of assistance in the way of joint development of fish processing facilities, and the purchase of sugar and timber at rates above current international market rates.

Soviet strategic and political objectives in the Pacific islands, as John Dorrance comments,[8] parallel those in many other regions: erosion of U.S. and other Western political influence, promotion of island state nonalignment, and restriction of U.S. regional naval and air access. On balance, the pursuit of these objectives thus far has been marked more by failure than success. The region's political and cultural environment is such that any future Soviet successes in these areas (in contrast to fisheries or other commercial arrangements) are likely to result primarily from Western indifference or insensitivity to the interests and concerns of the island states, and from the activity of regional Soviet surrogates (e.g., Marxist and other leftist Australian and New Zealand trade unions) and others who independently pursue objectives congruent with those of Moscow. Nevertheless, the United States and its regional friends and allies cannot afford to view with complaisance Soviet challenges to their interests in the Pacific islands.

New Soviet interest in the area has been paralleled by the growing presence or activity of other extra-regional states. Asian nations, such as the People's Republic of China, Taiwan, Japan, and the ASEAN states have all increased their diplomatic and/or economic presence. Libya was active in the region in the mid-1980s, particularly in Vanuatu and New Caledonia; Vanuatu sent personnel to Libya for "security and journalism" training. The European Community, West Germany, and Britain also have become more active in recent years, particularly in the area of development assistance.

The Importance of Economic Assistance

Although nearly all island states accept most fundamental Western strategic interests and requirements, their perceptions of their own strategic interests are far narrower. Perceiving few or no external military

---
[8] See above, pp. 66-92.

threats, their concerns are: the potential for political instability that flows from economic insecurity and the rising expectations of their peoples; the related inadequacies of development assistance and increasing aid dependency; associated perceptions of limits on their political freedom of action; external state insensitivity to their sovereignty (e.g., piracy of marine resources); insensitivity toward regional interests (e.g., Japanese and Taiwanese drift-net fishing and the U.S. failure to adhere to the SPNFZ protocols); past French colonial policies; and French nuclear testing. To the extent island governments perceive their interests are threatened by others, they are likely to be less sympathetic to the strategic requirements of the latter.

A major challenge for the island states is that of competition for an adequate share of finite global development assistance resources. Aside from their own need for higher levels, they face several fundamental problems. First, traditional Western donors increasingly face resource restraints of their own which limit the potential for increasing present levels of assistance—or even maintaining present levels. Second, the United States and European donors are faced with competing higher priorities, for example, aid to Eastern Europe. Third, a major political lever of the past is becoming increasingly ineffectual. To some degree U.S. (but also Australian) aid and other attention to the Pacific islands has been driven by a need to counter a perceived Soviet threat. Declining threat perceptions now assure lower levels of concern regarding Soviet activities. These factors give added weight to the importance of new sources of aid, for example, Japan, but also potentially some other Asian nations.

Hopefully, however, traditional donors will increasingly accept that their interests are well served by practical recognition of the uniqueness of the Pacific islands relative to other Third World regions. It is the only such region that generally shares and practices democratic and free enterprise values, and which gives full practical recognition to human rights. Fiji presently is an aberration, but hopefully a temporary one. Successful evolution of the political status of the French territories and Palau will eliminate the only remaining significant exceptions to independence or self-government. But, even with these exceptions, the region is blessed by an absence of single-party repressive dictatorial regimes, and of Marxist or other controlled economies. The ability of the island states to sustain this enviable record, and thus the prospects for a continuing pro-West orientation, is, however, in large degree dependent upon their ability to service the legitimate expectations of their peoples—a requirement that mandates continuing high levels of donor assistance, as well as concerted efforts to promote higher levels of private sector investment and trade, with the long-term objective of reducing levels of aid dependency.

Recommendations

Despite the previously mentioned erosion of goodwill toward the United States, the latter is still held in remarkably high regard within the region. Indeed, most island states seek higher levels of U.S. diplomatic presence and dialogue, U.S. investment and trade, and U.S. educational opportunities. In that context there were constructive adjustments in U.S. policy toward the South Pacific in 1988 and 1989. The U.S. diplomatic presence has been increased, a modest aid program has been expanded somewhat, and in general there has been a higher level of political attention, dialogue, and policy sensitivity. However, much remains to be done, and a small additional investment in sensitivity and resources can reap major dividends for U.S. and other Western interests.

Each of the contributors to these two volumes on the South Pacific not only has addressed the diverse forces shaping the future of the Pacific islands, but also has assessed policy implications and consequent options for the United States. Without suggesting that all authors would necessarily endorse each of the recommendations set forth below, an effort has been made to summarize the principal policy suggestions that emerge from the various chapters.

* High priority should be given by the United States to developing a more adequate understanding of the changing national aspirations of political leaders and other elites in the island states and remaining dependent territories.

* U.S. diplomatic activity in the South Pacific should include more frequent visits to the region by high-ranking U.S. officials, and more invitations to senior island state leaders to visit Washington. Of particular importance, the United States must (as it did in 1989) take full advantage of the South Pacific Forum's offer to join in a dialogue with Forum heads of government annually on the pattern of the ASEAN post-ministerial meetings.

* To promote greater understanding between societies, Washington should expand educational exchanges, as well as USIA programs which fund travel to the United States by island political, labor, academic, and media leaders.

* An effort should be made to increase and diversify trade between island states and the United States, including exploration of the possibility of "free-trade" entry into the United States of island state products on the pattern of Australia's and New Zealand's SPARTECA arrangement and the U.S. "Caribbean Initiative."

- Similarly, American private sector investment in the South Pacific should be encouraged through existing governmental mechanisms that have proved effective in other regions.

- Given the high level of Australia's and New Zealand's economic interests and involvement in South Pacific island states, major U.S. trade and investment initiatives should be developed in consultation with Canberra and Wellington.

- U.S. development assistance in the South Pacific should be increased modestly to match more nearly the level of U.S. strategic and political interests in that region. Current efforts to move away from regional projects to bilateral programs should be continued. That strategy is essential vis-a-vis island state sovereignty sensitivities and related U.S. political objectives.

- Regionalism and strong regional institutions well serve both regional state and Western interests. Although U.S. influence in this area is limited, initiatives that reinforce regional cohesion and cooperation should be encouraged and supported.

- In particular, the United States should take its participation in the South Pacific Commission more seriously with higher levels of representation and expertise.

- Island state internal stability crises may emerge in which a government may request external military assistance. In the South Pacific it is far more appropriate that Australian or New Zealand forces, rather than those of the United States or other major external powers, cope with such emergencies. However, in extreme cases, the United States should be prepared to provide logistics or other support, if requested.

- Limited U.S. defense cooperation with South Pacific island states possessing security forces should be continued, but not expanded to the point where it competes with Australian and New Zealand programs. U.S. military "civic action" public works projects and disaster relief are greatly appreciated by the island states and have had considerable favorable impact. These programs should be increased.

- Present efforts to maintain port and airfield access in the South Pacific are critical and should be continued through diplomatic and defense channels.

- Nuclear issues will remain a dominant regional concern requiring the utmost discretion and tact, including a periodic serious review by the United States of its position on adherence to the SPNFZ protocols.

- Moderate Western trade unions, but particularly those in Australia, New Zealand, and the United States, should be encouraged to increase their efforts to counter Marxist and other leftist trade unions operating in the Pacific islands as surrogates for the Soviets. Similarly, the International Confederation of Free Trade Unions should be encouraged to play a more active role in countering the regional activities of the World Federation of Trade Unions, a Soviet front organization.

- The issue of the future status of Palau, the last element of the Micronesian trusteeship to be "decolonized," should be resolved at an early date. While Palauans must resolve the constitutional issues blocking their preference for free association with the United States, the United States should seek ways to facilitate that process while protecting both Palauan and U.S. interests.

- Although the future of the U.S. territories (Guam and American Samoa) is not a regional decolonization issue, that could change in the absence of an adequate Washington response to Guam's desire for commonwealth status and higher levels of self-government, but for continuing U.S. sovereignty. U.S. interests, including that of support for the principle of self-determination, thus require early resolution of Guam's future status.

- To the extent practicable, and if desired by all parties, the United States could provide assistance to New Caledonia during its transition period. U.S. educational opportunities could be provided to New Caledonia's Kanaks, and U.S. investment in Kanak development projects in New Caledonia could be encouraged. These measures would help counter present negative Kanak images of the United States.

- The United States will be faced with an increasingly nationalistic and independent-minded Australia which also will become more and more important as a major regional power. Continued high levels of official dialogue will be of increasing importance to the relationship. However, that dialogue must be strengthened by still higher levels of effective public diplomacy directed at Australian public understanding of U.S. interests and positions, and of the importance of the alliance relationship to both nations.

- Mutual perceptions and understanding of the United States and Australia should be improved, both through new private-sector linkages (business councils and other nongovernmental binational cooperative bodies) and through support of American and Australian studies centers at universities in both countries.

- Despite New Zealand's disruption of the ANZUS alliance with its nuclear-free policies, U.S. and New Zealand interests and objectives in the South Pacific generally remain common or compatible. In these circumstances, U.S. policy goals in the region would be well served by restoration of normal diplomatic and other dialogue with Wellington, and closer cooperation in the South Pacific.

- The United States, Australia, France, and New Zealand should more closely coordinate their policies and actions in the region, and should seek to integrate Japan into these Western consultative processes.

- The Department of State should give higher priority to training specialists in Australian, New Zealand, and Pacific islands affairs, and to utilizing effectively these specialists up to the Deputy Assistant Secretary of State level. The establishment in 1989 of a Deputy Assistant Secretary position responsible for that region is a major organizational improvement with respect to management of U.S. relations with that region.

Summary

In sum, the Pacific islands, described by a diverse group of scholars and statesmen in these two volumes, represent a region of growing importance, but also of change and new challenges to traditional U.S. and other Western interests. The emergence of a galaxy of new states in the Pacific, and their relationship to critical sea and air lanes, will continue to heighten the salience of the region for the Pacific rim nations, and for other external powers.

From a Western perspective, change and challenge in the Pacific islands have not yet reached unmanageable proportions, especially since Western and regional state interests are generally compatible. But the potential for trouble is present as less conservative, and more ideologically motivated and assertive, island elites replace those who emerged in the immediate post-World War II period, as expectations out-pace economic development, and as the Soviets and some other external powers seek opportunities to challenge traditional Western influences.

If nothing else, change and challenge in the Pacific islands now require higher levels of Western state policy consultation and coordination, a continuing high level of development assistance, promotion of private sector trade and investment, and sustained higher levels of attention to and sensitivity toward regional state interests and concerns. The latter point particularly applies to the United States vis-a-vis the South Pacific.

Regional change also requires adjustment to new realities. The Western strategy of deterrence of conflict through alliance strength and cooperation will remain essential in the Pacific as elsewhere, but hopefully at less expensive and less threatening armament levels. In the Pacific islands context, that strategy will best be served by policies that promote a continuing pro-Western regional orientation, and the preservation of the region's exceptional record in the way of democratic institutions and respect for human rights. At the East-West level, a major challenge for the United States and its regional friends and allies will be to develop a strategy, which will channel diverse interests of states in the region in directions that mesh with broader strategies intended ultimately to integrate more fully the states of the South Pacific into the matrix of global political and economic processes.

The challenges are clear—but so are the opportunities to address those challenges.

BRASSEY'S (US), Inc.

List of Publications
published for the
Institute for Foreign Policy Analysis, Inc.

Orders for the following titles should be addressed to: Macmillan/Brassey's (US), Inc., Front and Brown Streets, Riverside, New Jersey 08075 (toll-free telephone number: 1-800-257-5755), or to Pergamon-Brassey's, Headington Hill Hall, Oxford, OX3 0BW, England.

Foreign Policy Reports

Ethics, Deterrence, and National Security. By James E. Dougherty, Midge Decter, Pierre Hassner, Laurence Martin, Michael Novak, and Vladimir Bukovsky. 1985. xvi, 91pp. $9.95.

American Sea Power and Global Strategy. By Robert J. Hanks. 1985. viii, 92pp. $9.95.

Decision-Making in Communist Countries: An Inside View. By Jan Sejna and Joseph D. Douglass, Jr. 1986. xii, 75pp. $9.95.

National Security: Ethics, Strategy, and Politics. A Layman's Primer. By Robert L. Pfaltzgraff, Jr. 1986. v, 37pp. $9.95.

Deterring Chemical Warfare: U.S. Policy Options for the 1990s. By Hugh Stringer. 1986. xii, 71pp. $9.95.

The Crisis of Communism: Its Meaning, Origins, and Phases. By Rett R. Ludwikowski. 1986. xii, 79pp. $9.95.

Transatlantic Discord and NATO's Crisis of Cohesion. By Peter H. Langer. 1986. viii, 89pp. $9.95.

The Reorganization of the Joint Chiefs of Staff: A Critical Analysis. Contributions by Allan R. Millett, Mackubin Thomas Owens, Bernard E. Trainor, Edward C. Meyer, and Robert Murray. 1986. xi, 67pp. $9.95.

The Soviet Perspective on the Strategic Defense Initiative. By Dmitry Mikheyev. 1987. xii, 88pp. $9.95.

On Guard for Victory: Military Doctrine and Ballistic Missile Defense in the USSR. By Steven P. Adragna. 1987. xiv, 87pp. $9.95.

Special Reports

Strategic Minerals and International Security. Edited by Uri Ra'anan and Charles M. Perry. 1985. viii, 85pp. $9.95.

Third World Marxist-Leninist Regimes: Strengths, Vulnerabilities, and U.S. Policy. By Uri Ra'anan, Francis Fukuyama, Mark Falcoff, Sam C. Sarkesian, and Richard H. Shultz, Jr. 1985. xv, 125pp. $9.95.

The Red Army on Pakistan's Border: Policy Implications for the United States. By Anthony Arnold, Richard P. Cronin, Thomas Perry Thornton, Theodore L. Eliot, Jr., and Robert L. Pfaltzgraff, Jr. 1986. vi, 83pp. $9.95.

Asymmetries in U.S. and Soviet Strategic Defense Programs: Implications for Near-Term American Deployment Options. By William A. Davis, Jr. 1986. xi, 71pp. $9.95.

Regional Security and Anti-Tactical Ballistic Missiles: Political and Technical Issues. By William A. Davis, Jr. 1986. xii, 54pp. $9.95.

Determining Future U.S. Tactical Airlift Requirements. By Jeffrey Record. 1987. vii, 40pp. $9.95.

Naval Forces and Western Security. By Francis J. West, Jr., Jacquelyn K. Davis, James E. Dougherty, Robert J. Hanks, and Charles M. Perry. 1987. xi, 56pp. $9.95.

NATO's Maritime Strategy: Issues and Developments. By. E.F. Gueritz, Norman Friedman, Clarence A. Robinson, and William R. Van Cleave. 1987. xii, 79pp. $9.95.

NATO's Maritime Flanks: Problems and Prospects. By H.F. Zeiner-Gundersen, Sergio A. Rossi, Marcel Duval, Donald C. Daniel, Gael D. Tarleton, and Milan Vego. 1987. xii, 119pp. $9.95.

SDI: Has America Told Her Story to the World? By Dean Godson. Report of the IFPA Panel on Public Diplomacy. 1987. xviii, 67pp. $9.95.

British Security Policy and the Atlantic Alliance: Prospects for the 1990s. By Martin Holmes, Gerald Frost, Christopher Coker, David Greenwood, Mark D.W. Edington, Dean Godson, Jacquelyn K. Davis, and Robert L. Pfaltzgraff, Jr. 1987. xv, 134pp. $9.95.

Nicaragua v. United States: A Look at the Facts. By Robert F. Turner. 1987. xiv, 159pp. $9.95.

The Grenada Documents: Window on Totalitarianism. By Nicholas Dujmovic. 1988. xiv, 88pp. $9.95.

American Military Policy in Small Wars: The Case of El Salvador. By A.J. Bacevich, James D. Hallums, Richard H. White, and Thomas F. Young. 1988. ix, 51pp. $9.95.

The U.S.-Korean Security Relationship: Prospects and Challenges for the 1990s. By Harold C. Hinton, Donald Zagoria, Jung Ha Lee, Gottfried-Karl Kindermann, Chung Min Lee, and Robert L. Pfaltzgraff, Jr. 1988. xi, 100pp. $9.95.

Security Perspectives of the West German Left: The SPD and the Greens in Opposition. By William E. Griffith, Werner Kaltefleiter, Edwina S. Campbell, Jan Erik Surotchak, Tamah Swenson, Jacquelyn K. Davis, and Robert L. Pfaltzgraff, Jr. 1988. xii, 126pp. $9.95.

The INF Controversy: Lessons for NATO Modernization and Transatlantic Relations. By Jacquelyn K. Davis, Charles M. Perry, and Robert L. Pfaltzgraff, Jr. 1989. xii, 119pp. $9.95.

The South Pacific: Political, Economic, and Military Trends. By Henry S. Albinski, Robert C. Kiste, Richard Herr, Ross Babbage, and Denis McLean. 1989. xiv, 100pp. $9.95.

Books

Atlantic Community in Crisis: A Redefinition of the Atlantic Relationship. Edited by Walter F. Hahn and Robert L. Pfaltzgraff, Jr. 1979. 386pp. $43.00.

Revising U.S. Military Strategy: Tailoring Means to Ends. By Jeffrey Record. 1984. 113pp. $16.95 ($9.95, paper).

Shattering Europe's Defense Consensus: The Antinuclear Protest Movement and the Future of NATO. Edited by James E. Dougherty and Robert L. Pfaltzgraff, Jr. 1985. 226pp. $18.95.

Selling the Rope to Hang Capitalism? The Debate on West-East Trade and Technology Transfer. Edited by Charles M. Perry and Robert L. Pfaltzgraff, Jr. 1987. xiii, 246pp. $30.00.

Why the Soviets Violate Arms Control Treaties. By Joseph D. Douglass, Jr. 1988. xiii, 202pp. $32.00.

Ending a Nuclear War: Are the Superpowers Prepared? Edited by Stephen J. Cimbala and Joseph D. Douglass, Jr. 1988. x, 198pp. $28.00.

INSTITUTE FOR FOREIGN POLICY ANALYSIS, INC.

List of Publications

Orders for the following titles in IFPA's series of Special Reports, Foreign Policy Reports, National Security Papers, Conference Reports, and Books should be addressed to the Circulation Manager, Institute for Foreign Policy Analysis, Central Plaza Building, Tenth Floor, 675 Massachusetts Avenue, Cambridge, Massachusetts 02139-3396. (Telephone: 617/492-2116.) Please send a check or money order for the correct amount together with your order.

Foreign Policy Reports

Defense Technology and the Atlantic Alliance: Competition or Collaboration? By Frank T.J. Bray and Michael Moodie. April 1977. vi, 42pp. $5.00.

Iran's Quest for Security: U.S. Arms Transfers and the Nuclear Option. By Alvin J. Cottrell and James E. Dougherty. May 1977. 59pp. $5.00.

Ethiopia, the Horn of Africa, and U.S. Policy. By John H. Spencer. September 1977. 69pp. $5.00.

Beyond the Arab-Israeli Settlement: New Directions for U.S. Policy in the Middle East. By R.K. Ramazani. September 1977. viii, 69pp. $5.00.

Spain, the Monarchy and the Atlantic Community. By David C. Jordan. June 1979. v, 55pp. $5.00.

U.S. Strategy at the Crossroads: Two Views. By Robert J. Hanks and Jeffrey Record. July 1982. viii, 69pp. $7.50.

The U.S. Military Presence in the Middle East: Problems and Prospects. By Robert J. Hanks. December 1982. vii, 77pp. $7.50.

Southern Africa and Western Security. By Robert J. Hanks. August 1983. vii, 71pp. $7.50.

The West German Peace Movement and the National Question. By Kim R. Holmes. March 1984. x, 73pp. $7.50.

The History and Impact of Marxist-Leninist Organizational Theory. By John P. Roche. April 1984. x, 70pp. $7.50.

Special Reports

The Cruise Missile: Bargaining Chip or Defense Bargain? By Robert L. Pfaltzgraff, Jr., and Jacquelyn K. Davis. January 1977. x, 53pp. $3.00.

Eurocommunism and the Atlantic Alliance. By James E. Dougherty and Diane K. Pfaltzgraff. January 1977. xiv, 66pp. $3.00.

The Neutron Bomb: Political, Technical and Military Issues. By S.T. Cohen. November 1978. xii, 95pp. $6.50.

SALT II and U.S.-Soviet Strategic Forces. By Jacquelyn K. Davis, Patrick J. Friel, and Robert L. Pfaltzgraff, Jr. June 1979. xii, 51pp. $5.00.

The Emerging Strategic Environment: Implications for Ballistic Missile Defense. By Leon Gouré, William G. Hyland, and Colin S. Gray. December 1979. xi, 75pp. $6.50.

The Soviet Union and Ballistic Missile Defense. By Jacquelyn K. Davis, Uri Ra'anan, Robert L Pfaltzgraff, Jr., Michael J. Deane, and John M. Collins. March 1980. xi, 71pp. $6.50. (Out of print).

Energy Issues and Alliance Relationships: The United States, Western Europe and Japan. By Robert L. Pfaltzgraff, Jr. April 1980. xii, 71pp. $6.50.

U.S. Strategic-Nuclear Policy and Ballistic Missile Defense: The 1980s and Beyond. By William Schneider, Jr., Donald G. Brennan, William A. Davis, Jr., and Hans Rühle. April 1980. xii, 61pp. $6.50.

The Unnoticed Challenge: Soviet Maritime Strategy and the Global Choke Points. By Robert J. Hanks. August 1980. xi, 66pp. $6.50.

Force Reductions in Europe: Starting Over. By Jeffrey Record. October 1980. xi, 91pp. $6.50.

SALT II and American Security. By Gordon J. Humphrey, William R. Van Cleave, Jeffrey Record, William H. Kincade, and Richard Perle. October 1980. xvi, 65pp.

The Future of U.S. Land-Based Strategic Forces. By Jake Garn, J.I. Coffey, Lord Chalfont, and Ellery B. Block. December 1980. xvi, 80pp.

The Cape Route: Imperiled Western Lifeline. By Robert J. Hanks. February 1981. xi, 80pp. $6.50 (Hardcover, $10.00).

Power Projection and the Long-Range Combat Aircraft: Missions, Capabilities and Alternative Designs. By Jacquelyn K. Davis and Robert L. Pfaltzgraff, Jr. June 1981. ix, 37pp. $6.50.

The Pacific Far East: Endangered American Strategic Position. By Robert J. Hanks. October 1981. vii, 75pp. $7.50.

NATO's Theater Nuclear Force Modernization Program: The Real Issues. By Jeffrey Record. November 1981. viii, 102pp. $7.50.

The Chemistry of Defeat: Asymmetries in U.S. and Soviet Chemical Warfare Postures. By Amoretta M. Hoeber. December 1981. xiii, 91pp. $6.50.

The Horn of Africa: A Map of Political-Strategic Conflict. By James E. Dougherty. April 1982. xv, 74pp. $7.50.

The West, Japan and Cape Route Imports: The Oil and Non-Fuel Mineral Trades. By Charles Perry. June 1982. xiv, 88pp. $7.50.

The Rapid Deployment Force and U.S. Military Intervention in the Persian Gulf. By Jeffrey Record. May 1983. Second Edition. viii, 83pp. $7.50.

The Greens of West Germany: Origins, Strategies, and Transatlantic Implications. By Robert L. Pfaltzgraff, Jr., Kim R. Holmes, Clay Clemens, and Werner Kaltefleiter. August 1983. xi, 105pp. $7.50.

The Atlantic Alliance and U.S. Global Strategy. By Jacquelyn K. Davis and Robert L. Pfaltzgraff, Jr. September 1983. x, 44pp. $7.50.

World Energy Supply and International Security. By Herman Franssen, John P. Hardt, Jacquelyn K. Davis, Robert J. Hanks, Charles Perry, Robert L. Pfaltzgraff, Jr., and Jeffrey Record. October 1983. xiv, 93pp. $7.50.

Poisoning Arms Control: The Soviet Union and Chemical/Biological Weapons. By Mark C. Storella. June 1984. xi, 99pp. $7.50.

National Security Papers

CBW: The Poor Man's Atomic Bomb. By Neil C. Livingstone and Joseph D. Douglass, Jr., with a Foreword by Senator John Tower. February 1984. x, 33pp. $5.00.

U.S. Strategic Airlift: Requirements and Capabilities. By Jeffrey Record. January 1986. vi, 38pp. $6.00.

Strategic Bombers: How Many Are Enough? By Jeffrey Record. January 1986. vi, 22pp. $6.00.

Strategic Defense and Extended Deterrence: A New Transatlantic Debate. By Jacquelyn K. Davis and Robert L. Pfaltzgraff, Jr. February 1986. viii, 51pp. $8.00.

JCS Reorganization and U.S. Arms Control Policy. By James E. Dougherty. March 1986. xiv, 27pp. $6.00.

Strategic Force Modernization and Arms Control. Contributions by Edward L. Rowny, R. James Woolsey, Harold Brown, Alexander M. Haig, Jr., Albert Gore, Jr., Brent Scowcroft, Russell E. Dougherty, A. Casey, Gordon Fornell, and Sam Nunn. 1986. xiii, 43pp. $6.00.

U.S. Bomber Force Modernization. Contributions by Mike Synar, Richard K. Betts, William Kaufmann, Russell E. Dougherty, Richard DeLauer, and Dan Quayle. 1986. vii, 9pp. $5.00.

U.S. Strategic Airlift Choices. Contributions by William S. Cohen, Russell Murray, Frederick G. Kroesen, William Kaufmann, Harold Brown, James A. Courter, and Robert W. Komer. 1986. ix, 13pp. $5.00.

Gorbachev's Afghan Gambit. By Theodore L. Eliot, Jr., 1988. vii, 19pp. $5.00.

Books

Soviet Military Strategy in Europe. By Joseph D. Douglass, Jr. Pergamon Press, 1980. 252pp. (Out of print).

The Warsaw Pact: Arms, Doctrine, and Strategy. By William J. Lewis. New York: McGraw-Hill Publishing Co., 1982. 471pp. $15.00.

The Bishops and Nuclear Weapons: The Catholic Pastoral Letter on War and Peace. By James E. Dougherty. Archon Books, 1984. 255pp. $22.50.

Conference Reports

NATO and Its Future: A German-American Roundtable. Summary of a Dialogue. 1978. 22pp. $1.00.

Second German-American Roundtable on NATO: The Theater-Nuclear Balance. 1978. 32pp. $1.00.

The Soviet Union and Ballistic Missile Defense. 1978. 26pp. $1.00.

U.S. Strategic-Nuclear Policy and Ballistic Missile Defense: The 1980s and Beyond. 1979. 30pp. $1.00.

SALT II and American Security. 1979. 39pp.

The Future of U.S. Land-Based Strategic Forces. 1979. 32pp. $1.00.

The Future of Nuclear Power. 1980. 48pp. $1.00.

Third German-American Roundtable on NATO: Mutual and Balanced Force Reductions in Europe. 1980. 27pp. $1.00.

Fourth German-American Roundtable on NATO: NATO Modernization and European Security. 1981. 15pp. $1.00.

Second Anglo-American Symposium on Deterrence and European Security. 1981. 25pp. $1.00.

The U.S. Defense Mobilization Infrastructure: Problems and Priorities. The Tenth Annual Conference, sponsored by the International Security Studies Program, The Fletcher School of Law and Diplomacy, Tufts University. 1981. 25pp. $1.00.

U.S. Strategic Doctrine for the 1980s. 1982. 14pp.

French-American Symposium on Strategy, Deterrence and European Security. 1982. 14pp. $1.00.

Fifth German-American Roundtable on NATO: The Changing Context of the European Security Debate. Summary of a Transatlantic Dialogue. 1982. 22pp. $1.00.

Energy Security and the Future of Nuclear Power. 1982. 39pp. $2.50.

International Security Dimensions of Space. The Eleventh Annual Conference, sponsored by the International Security Studies Program, The Fletcher School of Law and Diplomacy, Tufts University. 1982. 24pp. $2.50.

Portugal, Spain and Transatlantic Relations. Summary of a Transatlantic Dialogue. 1983. 18pp. $2.50.

Japanese-American Symposium on Reducing Strategic Minerals Vulnerabilities: Current Plans, Priorities, and Possibilities for Cooperation. 1983. 31pp. $2.50.

National Security Policy: The Decision-Making Process. The Twelfth Annual Conference, sponsored by the International Security Studies Program, The Fletcher School of Law and Diplomacy, Tufts University. 1983. 28pp. $2.50.

The Security of the Atlantic, Iberian and North African Regions. Summary of a Transatlantic Dialogue. 1983. 25pp. $2.50.

The West European Antinuclear Protest Movement: Implications for Western Security. Summary of a Transatlantic Dialogue. 1984. 21pp. $2.50.

The U.S.-Japanese Security Relationship in Transition. Summary of a Transpacific Dialogue. 1984. 23pp. $2.50.

Sixth German-American Roundtable on NATO: NATO and European Security—Beyond INF. Summary of a Transatlantic Dialogue. 1984. 31pp. $2.50.

Security Commitments and Capabilities: Elements of an American Global Strategy. The Thirteenth Annual Conference, sponsored by the International Security Studies Program, The Fletcher School of Law and Diplomacy, Tufts University. 1984. 21pp. $2.50.

Third Japanese-American-German Conference on the Future of Nuclear Energy. 1984. 40pp. $2.50.

Seventh German-American Roundtable on NATO: Political Constraints, Emerging Technologies, and Alliance Strategy. Summary of a Transatlantic Dialogue. 1985. 36pp. $2.50.

Terrorism and Other "Low-Intensity" Operaions: International Linkages. The Fourteenth Annual Conference, sponsored by the International Security Studies Program, The Fletcher School of Law and Diplomacy, Tufts University. 1985. 21pp. $2.50.

East-West Trade and Technology Transfer: New Challenges for the United States. Second Annual Forum, co-sponsored by the Institute for Foreign Policy Analysis and the International Security Studies Program, The Fletcher School of Law and Diplomacy, Tufts University. 1986. 40pp. $3.50.

Organizing for National Security: The Role of the Joint Chiefs of Staff. 1986. 32pp. $2.50.

Eighth German-American Roundtable on NATO: Strategic Defense, NATO Modernization, and East-West Relations. Summary of a Transatlantic Dialogue. 1986. 47pp. $2.50.

Emerging Doctrines and Technologies: Implications for Global and Regional Political-Military Balances. The Fifteenth Annual Conference, sponsored by the International Security Studies Program, The Fletcher School of Law and Diplomacy, Tufts University. 1986. 49pp. $2.50.

Strategic War Termination: Political-Military-Diplomatic Dimensions. 1986. 22pp. $2.50.

SDI and European Security: Enhancing Conventional Defense. 1987. 21pp. $2.50.

Strategic Defense: Industrial Applications and Political Implications. 1987. ix, 29pp. $2.50.

The Future of NATO Forces. 1987. xi, 37pp. $2.50.

Protracted Warfare—The Third World Arena: A Dimension of U.S.-Soviet Conflict. The Sixteenth Annual Conference, sponsored by the International Security Studies Program, The Fletcher School of Law and Diplomacy, Tufts University. 1987. xi, 37pp. $2.50.

Ninth German-American Roundtable on NATO: NATO Modernization, Arms Control, and East-West Relations. Summary of a Transatlantic Dialogue. 1988. vii, 68pp. $2.50.

Third International Roundtable Conference: East-West Relations in the 1990s—Politics and Technology. 1988. v, 48pp. $2.50.

Strategic Defense Initiative: The First Five Years. 1988. xiv, 90pp. $2.50.

Fourth International Roundtable Conference: The Atlantic Alliance and Western Security as NATO Turns Forty—Setting the Agenda. 1989. v, 54pp. $2.50.